Subject Leadership in the Primary School

A Practical Guide for Curriculum Coordinators

JOAN DEAN

David Fulton Publishers

London

David Fulton Publishers
2 Park Square, Milton Park, Abingdon, Oxon OX14 4RN

270 Madison Avenue, New York, NY 10016

First published in 2003
Transferred to digital printing

David Fulton Publishers is an imprint of the Taylor & Francis Group, an informa business

Copyright © Joan Dean 2003

The right of Joan Dean to be identified as the author of this work has been asserted by her in accordance with the Copyright, Designs and Patents Act 1988.

British Library Cataloguing in Publication Data
A catalogue record for this book is available from the British Library.

ISBN 1-84312-083-6

Typeset by Kenneth Burnley, Wirral, Cheshire

Contents

CHAPTER 1

Introduction

In today's primary schools almost every teacher is likely to be in a leadership role. Teachers are leaders in their own classrooms in any case, and in larger schools there may be teachers with responsibility for coordinating the work of a Key Stage or a year group but the demand for subject coordination or leadership means that almost everyone will be a subject leader for at least one subject, and in a small school subject leaders may be responsible for two or even more subjects. You may therefore find yourself advising colleagues with far more teaching experience than you have. You may also not be a trained specialist in the subject you have been asked to lead and will need to attend courses in order to learn about the job. It is also the case that there is little allowance for non-contact time in primary schools and this makes the task even more difficult. Being a subject leader is not an easy task, but it is a very rewarding one in which you can really make a difference to what is happening in your school.

Those in subject leadership posts are often called 'subject coordinator'. Bell and Ritchie suggest that:

> The term subject leader suggests a more proactive approach that anticipates events, plans for improvement and creates opportunities to increase the effectiveness of teaching in the subject and pupils' learning across the whole school. The term coordinator tends to imply a position that is passive and reactive to the responsibilities and opportunities that present themselves. (1999:10)

The role has changed over recent years and the term 'subject leader' now seems to be the more appropriate one. The National Standards for Subject Leaders describe the core purpose of the subject leader as being:

> To provide professional leadership and management for a subject to secure high quality teaching, effective use of resources and improved standards of learning and achievement for all pupils. (Teacher Training Agency 1998:4)

It goes on to note that 'a subject leader plays a key role in supporting, guiding and motivating teachers of the subject and other adults'.

A good school with a good head teacher tries to empower its staff. Starratt suggests that a school which is empowering its members manages three things:

1. each person finds a personally fulfilling way of exercising his or her unique talents in the pursuit of common ideas and ideals;
2. members of the community are able to achieve things that they could not achieve on their own; and
3. the power of the ideas and ideals raises people's abilities to a new level and gives a focus and an intensity to their activities that they would not have without those ideas and ideals. (1995:39)

He also suggests that:

> Leadership emerges out of a vision of what the leader and the colleagues can accomplish. The vision embraces an ideal, a dream that is grounded in those fundamental meanings and values that feed a sense of human fulfilment. The compelling power of leadership flows from a shared vision. (1995:14)

As a subject leader you have to be both a leader and a manager. Leaders are concerned with developing and communicating vision, inspiration and the direction which results from these. Managers are concerned with making and implementing plans, setting up systems, managing resources, and are accountable for getting things done. Both aspects of the role require you to work effectively with people.

A number of writers speak of transactional and transformational leadership. Terrell describes transformational leaders:

> Leaders who 'transform' are good at establishing and communicating values and beliefs. They communicate aims and directions and have a strong sense of vision. These form the basis of setting long-term goals, which are reduced down to specific and individual short-term goals. (1997:103)

Transformational leadership is leadership which works with and through other people, helping them to develop their values, achieve goals and fulfil a vision. It should help to empower them to develop their own skills of leadership in the classroom. Transactional leadership is leadership in which colleagues negotiate their individual interests with their leader as opposed to group interests. Both types of leadership may be needed.

The role of the subject leader

Bell and Ritchie suggest that:

1. the aim of effective curriculum leadership and coordination, regardless of subject area, is to provide the best possible learning opportunities for children in the school at any given time;

2. the post of coordinator is a rapidly evolving and complex one which requires extending professional and personal development into new areas, particularly those of leadership and management. (1999:2)

Schools make use of subject expertise in various ways. OFSTED surveys, not very surprisingly, suggest that the teaching of specialists in a subject is better than that of other teachers. With this in view some schools work on the basis that subject specialists teach their subject to more than one class. This is not easy to do, particularly in a small school which is staffed on the basis of one teacher per class, but some schools arrange specialist teaching, often in Years 5 and 6, by teachers exchanging classes. Another kind of organisation is one in which the specialist teaches a block of work with a particular class over a short period of time each term, either by the exchange of classes or because the head teacher or a supply teacher covers for the specialist. This sort of arrangement is unlikely to cover all the teaching of the subject, except perhaps in music where a specialist part-time teacher may be employed.

In most schools, at least some of the subject leader's task will be that of supporting and helping colleagues with their teaching of the subject. Once again, time for this may be made available by some employment of supply cover or by the head teacher covering for your class while you help a colleague. This is likely to be very limited since every subject leader needs this kind of opportunity. Much of your influence is likely to be through discussion with colleagues and advice and suggestions to help them with their teaching.

As subject leader you must first of all get to know the subject well, be familiar with the major concepts it involves, the evidence used, the skills it requires and the way in which this knowledge and these skills can best be taught. You need to keep up to date with developments both in the subject itself and in knowledge of ways of teaching it. You will then be in a position to advise colleagues about it. You also need to be knowledgeable about ways of using ICT to support your subject teaching. Your responsibilities are likely to include the following:

- auditing the current state of the subject;
- developing with colleagues a vision of what the school might achieve in the subject in the future;
- the development of policies and schemes of work in consultation with colleagues;
- planning with colleagues for the development of work in the subject and contributing to the school development plan;
- identifying aims and setting objectives for work in the subject;
- providing guidance on learning and teaching methods in the subject;

- supporting colleagues in their work in the classroom with advice and guidance and sometimes working alongside them;
- leading discussion about work in the subject;
- providing for the professional development of colleagues in their work in your subject and feeding back to them what you have learned in courses you have attended;
- helping colleagues with the differentiation of work to provide for children of different abilities and different backgrounds;
- taking responsibility for resources for the subject and ensuring that there are satisfactory systems for their use;
- helping colleagues to develop literacy, numeracy and ICT skills through the subject;
- ensuring a safe working and learning environment;
- evaluating what is happening in work in the subject at regular intervals;
- encouraging colleagues to engage in action research to develop their work and providing opportunities for teachers to share good practice;
- supporting newly qualified teachers as they develop work in your subject;
- working with relevant classroom assistants to enable them to contribute to work in the subject;
- undertaking relevant administrative tasks as they affect work in the subject;
- keeping the head teacher, governors and parents informed about work in the subject;
- liaising where appropriate with teachers in neighbouring primary schools, subject specialists in secondary schools and specialist advisers and inspectors.

Leaders have to manage both tasks and people, and both elements of the job are equally important. If you emphasise the importance of the task without taking into account the way people may be feeling about it, you are unlikely to be successful. Equally, if you are so concerned with the way people are feeling that the task does not get done, you will not succeed.

Good leaders need to be concerned with the motivation of those they lead and use that motivation to achieve good teaching. Frase and Conley suggest that 'motivated teachers are enthusiastic, skilled, happy to share knowledge and wisdom with their learners, and happy to share their success with their fellow teachers' (1994:16). Teachers are likely to be motivated by the following:

- Children developing and learning. Most teachers gain satisfaction from seeing that a child has learned something or acquired a new skill as a result of the teacher's efforts. There is also the longer-term satisfaction of seeing a child develop.

- Enthusiasm for subject matter. The teacher who really cares about the material he or she is teaching will be stimulated to maintain skill and knowledge and is more likely to inspire children.
- Recognition, interest, encouragement, praise. Providing these is an important part of the leadership role.
- A chance to contribute and to shine. People enjoy gaining recognition for the contribution they make to the group.
- A chance to take responsibility. Opportunities for this should be widely distributed.
- A challenge to professional skill. Problem-solving in situations which demand skills which you possess is very satisfying. Many teachers will rise to the challenge posed by a difficult pupil or a request to work at some new task.
- The inspiration of others. One of the main benefits of working collaboratively as a team is the opportunity for people to inspire each other.

To be a good leader you need to be positive and enthusiastic and convey this enthusiasm to others. You need to be clear about where you see the work in the subject going and how you might get there with the support of colleagues, but realistic about what can be achieved. You need to make others feel valued, thanking them for their contributions, praising and celebrating their achievements. You need to be a good listener, sensitive to other people, encouraging others to voice their ideas and drawing together the ideas which are put forward. Good leaders are not afraid of differences of opinion, recognising that they can be profitable when good new ways forward come out of this kind of discussion. You need to be ready to take decisions but involve other people in putting their views forward before arriving at a conclusion. You need to be honest, not afraid to admit mistakes, ready to take advice and ready to support other people.

You will need a range of leadership and management skills as a subject leader. You will need to be a good communicator, both in person and in writing. You need administrative and organisational skills both in dealing with colleagues and in managing resources. You will, from time to time, need to be decisive and make wise judgements, but able to do this sensitively and fairly. You need to be a good problem-solver. You need to be able to lead group discussion, handling conflict in the group constructively and leading it to conclusions which are workable. You will need the skills of motivating, counselling, advising, encouraging, mentoring, coaching, monitoring. You also need to be good at managing your own time and dealing with a measure of stress, able to give and receive criticism in a constructive way. In particular, you need a sense of humour.

One particular set of skills which will be important in making the job manageable involves assertiveness – the ability to say what you want in a clear and confident manner but without upsetting other people. Subject leaders may have to deal with other people being aggressive or trying to get their own way without regard for others, or passive in letting other people do what they want regardless. As a leader you need to encourage assertive behaviour in colleagues, recognising that people who suppress what they feel may at a later stage become aggressive. It is better to express clearly one's feelings and beliefs in a direct and honest way. A person acting assertively will make clear statements, distinguish between fact and opinion, seek the opinions of others and look for ways of resolving problems.

As a leader you will probably work in different styles according to the circumstances. Occasionally you will need to use a directive approach, but more often your approach will be open and democratic. This is especially important since effective leadership is dependent on carrying people with you. You need to be supportive, to involve people and bring together the best ideas, building strong bonds between you and using these for the benefit of the school. This kind of leadership is known to bring out the best in other people. Rodd (1994) writes of the motivator style of leadership which has the following characteristics:

- warmth and flexibility;
- sensitivity, creativity and encouragement;
- confidence in the abilities of colleagues and their commitment to hard work;
- supportive and non-judgemental;
- open, two-way communication channels;
- involvement and participation of colleagues in goal-setting and other important tasks;
- confident decision-making and problem-solving;
- frequent feedback;
- encouragement of self-evaluation and risk-taking.

The long-term aim of all the work with colleagues is the better learning of the children. Being a subject leader is about helping colleagues to teach to the best of their ability. The findings of various researchers suggest that effective teachers have the following characteristics:

- They prepare well and have clear goals for their teaching.
- They aim to make as much teaching contact with all their children as possible.
- They have high expectations for all children and communicate this well.
- They make clear presentations which match the age and ability level of the children.

- They structure work well and tell the children the purpose of the work they are doing and the goals they hope the children will achieve.
- They are flexible and vary their teaching behaviour and activities to match the subject matter and the needs of the children.
- They use many higher order questions which demand thinking on the part of the children.
- They give frequent feedback to children about how they are doing.
- They make appropriate use of praise for both achievement and behaviour.
- They keep good records of the attainment and progress of individual children and these are shared and used. Progress in learning is constantly assessed.
- Their classrooms are well organised, ordered and attractive.
- They reflect on the work they and the children have done and evaluate progress towards goals.

The work of such teachers should lead to effective learning by children which sets them on the road to becoming educated individuals who have learned how to learn and who enjoy the learning process and want to go on learning all their lives. They will be able to learn from observation, from discussion and questioning and from books and other sources. They will be good communicators, both verbally and in writing. They will be able to solve problems of many kinds. They will enjoy the arts and take pleasure in fine craftsmanship. They will care for the environment and feel responsibility towards it. They will be sensitive to others, understanding and caring in their attitudes and able to work in collaboration with them. They will grow up to be good citizens and good human beings.

QUESTIONS FOR CONSIDERATION

1 How well do I know my subject? Is my knowledge up to date?

2 How well do I teach my subject? How does my teaching measure up to the list of effective teaching styles given above?

3 Would I be happy to have other teachers observe my teaching?

4 What is my main motivation in teaching?

5 How do my skills measure up to the tasks in my job description?

6 Have I good organisational and administrative skills?

7 Am I good at problem-solving?

8 Am I able to give and receive criticism?

9 What is my preferred leadership style?

CHAPTER 2

Assessing the situation

CASE STUDY

Rose was in her fourth year of teaching when she was appointed to a post as a teacher of Year 3 and subject coordinator for geography. Geography had been her main degree subject and she enjoyed teaching it and looked forward to a leadership role in her new post.

After the interview the head teacher explained to her that geography in the school was something of a cause for concern. A recent OFSTED inspection had highlighted the inadequacy of work in the subject which had been led by a teacher who had now retired and who was in no way a geography specialist. There was much to be done.

Rose's first task, before term began, was to look at the documentation for the subject which had been forwarded to her. The scheme of work was sketchy and out of date and would need rewriting. The school had a general learning and teaching policy which she could go along with and find ways of applying it in geography teaching. There was also a list of the books and equipment which were available and this provision was also not very adequate.

When term began, Rose took early opportunities to talk to colleagues about how they viewed the teaching of geography. There was not much enthusiasm for the subject and several spoke of the pressures of the literacy and numeracy strategies making it difficult to give enough attention to other subjects. There had not been much discussion about how geography was to be taught and they each got on with it in their own classes. She looked round the classrooms with agreement from the teachers and found very little evidence of work in geography in the work displayed. She asked to see children's exercise books with work in geography and again found this very limited.

Rose's task now was to think how she could change the situation and stimulate an enthusiasm for this subject.

When you start in a new job as a subject leader in a new school you first of all need to find out a number of general things about the school as a background to work in your subject. What is the social background of the school? How many children are there who do not have English as their first language? How many children have special educational needs? How is the school organised – is there setting for some subjects? These pieces of information are likely to have been made available to you when you were appointed to your post. You will also get an impression of pupil behaviour from walking around the school.

Your next task, whether you are working in a new school or starting to undertake a new responsibility in your existing school, is to find out all you can about what is expected of you. Your first piece of information should be a job description. This may be individual to your subject or a more general document. It should state the tasks and responsibilities you will be expected to undertake and to whom and for whom you will be responsible for these. It should tell you how you are expected to fulfil your responsibilities, whether you are expected to do some specialist teaching or work with and through other teachers to develop the teaching of your subject. Other relevant documentation will be any policies about the teaching of the subject or more general policies about teaching and learning and any schemes of work. Do these seem to be appropriate and up to date? Do they meet the statutory requirements of the subject? Discussion with teachers and observation about the school will tell you whether the schemes are being followed and what effect they have had on practice in classrooms.

You need to give thought at an early stage to the ways in which you are going to set about auditing what has been happening in your subject area as a preliminary to making plans for its development. Your head teacher should be a valuable source of information about how the subject has been taught in the school and how your predecessor has worked. There may also be evidence from an OFSTED inspection and if your subject is English, mathematics or science there will be SATs results to guide you. How do these compare with those of other schools in the area or other schools nationally? Given the background of the school, do these results seem to be appropriate? You also need to ask questions about whether the SATs results show any significant differences between boys and girls and between children of different ethnic background. In other subjects there should be teacher assessments which will give you some information about the standards teachers believe the children are achieving.

If you have had the opportunity to talk with your predecessor, this too will be helpful in finding out how the subject has been led. You need to find out how much time teachers are expected to give to your subject and whether this works out in practice. It will be useful to know what meetings have been held to discuss the teaching of the subject and whether the policies and schemes of work have been the outcomes of discussion or imposed. You also need to know what part ICT has played in the teaching of your subject, what software has been made available and what skills the teachers and children have in using ICT. Your head teacher or predecessor may be prepared to tell you where there is strength and where there are problems in the teaching of the subject and offer advice on the best way to tackle them.

It will be important to talk with individual teachers and find out how they view their work in your subject. What seems to go well in the classroom? How do they regard the scheme of work? Is it useful or simply another piece of paper? How confident do they feel in teaching the subject? What problems are they finding? What help would they welcome? What are their concerns in the subject? You also need to find out how teachers like to organise their classrooms and their teaching. Is there any collaborative group work? What whole-class teaching takes place? What use is made of ICT and how might this be used in the future? What part does investigation play? How do they organise resources within their classrooms? Classroom assistants may also have valuable insights into what is happening in the school, especially the learning support assistants working with children with special educational needs.

Garrett makes the following comment which may be relevant in deciding how to go about helping people:

> An understanding of what makes people 'tick' can help to identify additional strategies for providing support where needed, helping to build confidence, working together and sharing hopes and concerns, all are recognised remedies for the difficulties of the transition culture. (1997:111)

You may find it helpful to ask colleagues to let you see their plans of work for the previous year or get them to complete a questionnaire giving the ground they have covered in your subject over the past term. Talking to children may also be useful and you will get an impression as to how they view work in your subject. You might ask Years 5 and 6 to write something for you about the work they have done in your subject over the past term.

It is also helpful to sample children's work. Ask each teacher to let you have a sample of work from one of the most able children, one of middle ability and one who is a slow learner. This will give you a picture of the situation over the school as a whole and will also give you clues about the way teachers are going about marking children's work. Are there agreed forms of assessment and a school assessment policy? Is the policy followed?

You may also find it useful to look at children's records, both at a school level and those of individual teachers if they are willing to let you see them. What sorts of things are being recorded? Is the system comprehensive and diagnostic? Does it provide the opportunity to identify children's difficulties and plan for them?

You will need to give some thought to the ways in which teachers might differentiate work for children of different abilities. How many children are there in the school with statements of special educational needs and what provision is made for them? What sort of provision is needed for such children in the teaching of your subject? Is anything special done to support children who show exceptional ability? How would you recognise and cater for exceptional ability in your subject?

Another source of information is the school development plan and any subject development plan which has stemmed from it. This will give you a picture of how the subject has been developed in the past and provide a starting point for your work in the school.

It may also be helpful to talk to other subject leaders about how they go about the tasks involved. What meetings do they have when they can talk with colleagues about the teaching of the subject? How do they monitor work? Do they have opportunities to visit other teachers and see how work is progressing in classrooms? It may also be helpful to find out where work in other subjects relates to your work. For example, opportunities for developing work in English and mathematics occur in many other subjects. History and geography and to some extent religious education have some things in common and it may be helpful to identify areas where you have common aims.

An important task for the newly appointed subject leader will be to review the resources available for the subject and find out how they are used. Is there an inventory of what is available and is this given to all teachers so that they know what is there? Is there a central collection or is most of the material in individual classrooms? How often is the resource bank checked to see if everything is there? If there is a central collection is there a system for borrowing from it and does this work satisfactorily? How much is the resource bank used? Are there gaps in resourcing? What opportunities for using ICT resources are available and how much are they used? How much was spent on this subject last year? What are the arrangements for budgeting and are these adequate? Do you need to make a case for exceptional spending on this subject in the next year? You will also need to look at how resources are cared for. How are they stored? Are they in suitable containers? What arrangements are made for checking that resources borrowed are returned intact? Who is responsible for seeing that anything broken is mended or repaired? You may be able to enlist the help of teacher assistants for this task.

In addition to displays in classrooms there may be opportunities for subject displays about the school. This is a useful way of stimulating interest in the subject for teachers and children and any visitors to the school.

You may also like to enquire about outside contacts in relation to your subject. Is there any contact with the specialist teachers in the secondary schools to which the children transfer? Is there an adviser in your subject in the area? Are there any groups of teachers from local schools meeting to discuss the teaching of your subject? Do subject leaders have an opportunity to talk to governors about their subject? Are there any opportunities to talk to a parents' meeting?

You also need to ask questions about the professional development opportunities in your subject which have been available to teachers. Have there been any in-service days in which the subject has been discussed? Have any teachers attended courses in the subject? How does the head teacher view providing opportunities for subject development as part of the school's in-service provision?

Finally it may be helpful at an early stage to find out what support you can expect in your subject role. Does the performance management system of the school involve regular reviews of the work of staff? Does your head teacher seem supportive of your role? Will there be any non-contact time for making observations of work or working alongside other teachers? Will you have any support from a classroom assistant? What clerical support will be available if needed? What opportunities will you have for your own development?

QUESTIONS FOR CONSIDERATION

1 Have I now obtained a clear picture of what has been happening in my subject?

2 What are the current standards of work at each stage in the school?

3 How do teachers view this subject?

4 What are the strengths of the subject in the school?

5 What problems and difficulties are there? Can I see any ways of dealing with these?

6 Are teachers in the habit of discussing teaching and learning?

7 How open are my colleagues about what is happening in their classrooms? What monitoring takes place in other subjects? What opportunities will I have for monitoring work in my subject?

8 What teaching approaches are staff using for this subject? Are they appropriate?

9 What provision is there for differentiating work to cater for children of varying abilities?

10 How does the school provide for children with statements of special educational needs? For very able children?

11 How do the children appear to view work in this subject?

12 What resources are available for the subject? How well are they organised? What opportunities are there likely to be for increasing them? What use is being made of ICT?

13 What professional development opportunities in the subject area have been made available to staff? What opportunities are there likely to be in the future?

14 What records are being kept in this subject? How useful are they?

15 What do my colleagues expect of me as subject leader?

16 What support can I expect as subject leader? From the head teacher? From teaching assistants? From office staff?

CHAPTER 3

Culture and vision

Every school has its own culture – 'the way we do things here'. Telford says of the school culture:

> It is a strong current which flows beneath the surface, giving meaning to and shaping the daily choices and priorities of school activities. It brings a propelling power to the decisions being made in the school, and yet it is largely unarticulated. (1996:87)

A view of the school culture is passed on to new staff members and to children by existing staff both formally and informally. It may be expressed in many ways. It will be formally expressed through statements of aims and objectives, descriptions of the curriculum, policy statements, organisational structures, rules, sanctions and rewards. There will informal expression of the culture in the way people react to situations and ideas and the things they demonstrate that they value. Children too will be part of the culture as teachers make them aware of the way they should do things in school. They also have a culture of their own, particularly in the older years.

As a subject leader you have to recognise the culture and look at ways in which it will support you in what you want to do and ways in which you would like to change it. Because the cultural norms are often largely unarticulated, you may be only vaguely aware of them, unless you are new to the school when you will be conscious of the ways in which the culture differs from the culture in your previous school. Yet your awareness of the culture is very important in the influence it will have on the way you set about working with your colleagues.

Busher and Harris make the following statement about culture:

> Not only is culture created by a group of staff but it also reflects the history of that group and how it has developed through coping with a series of situations. It creates for its members a lens through which every aspect of school life is likely to be perceived. Sharing a group culture leads to membership of the group who created it. Rejecting the culture means, for a member of staff, placing him- or herself outside that group.

> New staff in a school have to be taught the appropriate culture of the school and the sub-culture of its subject areas to help them belong. New members may also influence the culture. (2000:125, 126)

Glatthorn suggests that there are three key aspects of culture: 'the *belief system*, the core values and the guiding beliefs that inform action; the *norms*, the shared standards of behaviour that derive from the belief system; and the *traditions*, the valued ways of the past' (1990:58).

He goes on to say that culture may account for why some schools are more successful than others. It can lead to a consensus about goals which facilitates rational planning. Research suggests that the kind of culture which supports school improvement has the following characteristics:

- Members of the school community work together and trust each other. Teachers try to help and support each other, and leadership at all levels is seen as supportive rather than evaluative.
- Everyone is concerned with learning. Teachers and support staff see themselves as learners and expect to learn new things and new ways of working as part of their professional development as well as being concerned with the learning of pupils.
- The staff have common goals which have been discussed and agreed.
- People work together to solve problems and look for ways forward. The problems of individuals are seen as problems for the group.
- People are ready to experiment, try out ideas and discuss and share the results. New ideas are well received by those in leadership roles.
- People hold high expectations of each other and of the children.
- People are given recognition by their colleagues for their achievements.
- Children are encouraged to see learning as something desirable in its own right, not as a competition with others to see who can do the best.

The culture of a school stems from the values and beliefs of those who work there. The head teacher's values and beliefs will have a particular effect on the culture, but everyone's beliefs and values contribute. You need to discover how your colleagues think about children. What do they believe are the most important things the school should do? How do they believe children should be treated at school? How should teachers deal with children's behaviour? How friendly should they be? What do colleagues believe about the way children learn? How do they discover what children know? What is the best way of teaching them? How should children acquire social skills? How should they learn how to learn? What sorts of relationships with other teachers and teaching assistants do teachers value and feel are important? Do teachers believe in working together? Are they ready to help each other? Do they give recognition to each other's achievements? How do they deal with problems which occur? Do they share them and try to help each other? Are they still learners? How do they feel about the way the school runs? How do they feel about your subject?

If you are working in a school with the kind of culture described above you are fortunate because it will support your efforts to develop work in your subject area. If the culture is a rather different one where teachers tend to isolate themselves in their own classrooms you may need to work to persuade people to work together and support each other. This means trying to change the culture, at least so far as work in your subject is concerned. To do this you need to understand the culture that exists and the beliefs which support it, working in discussion with individuals and groups to find out what makes people 'tick'. It may be helpful to talk about this with other subject leaders to see whether they are happy with the existing culture or would like to work more cooperatively. You then need to work together to develop a vision of the future which involves developing a positive kind of culture in which there is a collegiate approach. Fleming and Amesbury describe a collegiate approach as one 'likely to generate a collaborative ethos, characterised by a clear vision, staff involvement in decision making and a culture of critical reflection, learning from peers and professional development' (2001:39).

They go on to say:

> Such a culture is most likely to be created by managers who show a genuine interest in team members, keep people informed and seek their opinions, stay calm and remain positive, are fair, lead by example, smile and praise and publicly and sincerely celebrate the successes of team members. (55)

The school vision needs to be summed up in a mission statement which gives a brief outline of the beliefs and values which the school supports.

CASE STUDY

Roberta was in her fifth year of teaching in the same school when she was asked to take over as subject leader for science. It had been her main degree subject and she had found the leadership in the subject very frustrating in the past because the teacher leading the subject had given very little direction or support to colleagues in their teaching of this subject. As a consequence there was a lack of progression and continuity and teachers did not know what children coming into their classes had done previously.

Teachers in some other subjects were used to working together, and the head teacher, who had been concerned about results in science in the past, was happy to allow Roberta to lead a staff meeting to discuss the teaching of science in the school.

She started by asking the teachers what developments they would most like to see in the teaching of science in the school. A number of suggestions were put forward. In particular they wanted a scheme of work which they could all use to guide their work and ensure progression. There were a number of suggestions about resources and some of the staff felt they still lacked knowledge of the subject and needed more in-service training.

She then asked them to work in pairs to set down the developments they would most like to see if they were to visit the school in three years' time. They then shared their ideas and Roberta was able to see which ideas seemed to be most important to her colleagues. At the end of the meeting she took their lists away and combined them into one statement which she brought back to them at a later meeting. This was discussed in detail and some changes made before a revised version was finally adopted as the programme for them all to work towards. The next step would be to discuss how this vision statement might be achieved.

Once you have become familiar with the culture in which you are working, your task is to develop a vision for work in your subject, working with your colleagues so that they share the vision and enthusiastically make it their own. This requires opportunities for discussion so that people can contribute to the vision, perhaps in the way suggested in the case study above. Starratt makes the following points about discussion of vision:

> The point is to keep the vision close to the conscious, everyday awareness of the teachers, not as a formula for orthodoxy, but as a dream that is capable of taking many shapes and forms . . . Leaders above all must be reflective. contemplative, meditative people. (1995:21)

Bennis and Nanus describe vision as:

> A mental image of a positive and desirable future state . . . as vague as a dream or as precise as a goal or mission statement . . . a vision of a realistic, credible, attractive future for the organisation, a condition that is better in some important ways than what now exists. (1985:174)

It will be important to try to make your vision statement as the outcome of all the discussion, brief and to the point so that people can keep it in mind as they work. It should provide answers to the question, 'Where are we going?', which leads to another question, 'Where are we now?' and the further question, 'How do we get there?' You also need to involve your head teacher in your plans for developing the vision of the staff for your subject. He or she will have a vision for the school which may or may not be articulated, and your plans will need to fit with this.

In addition to the vision that you work out with your colleagues, you will have your own vision of the way you would like them to work with you. It is worth trying to write this down so that you can keep it in mind and periodically assess progress towards it. Little lists the following factors which contribute to school improvement and which form a good basis for a personal vision for working with colleagues:

> Teachers engage in frequent, continuous and increasingly precise *talk* about teaching practice . . . By such talk, teachers build up a shared language adequate to the complexity of teaching, capable of distinguishing one practice and its virtue from another.

> Teachers . . . frequently *observe* each other teaching, and provide each other with useful (if potentially frightening) evaluations of their teaching.

> Teachers . . . *plan, design, research, evaluate and prepare teaching materials together.*

> Teachers . . . *teach each other* the practice of teaching. (1981:12, 13)

It will be important to ensure that the vision is one that can be achieved in the real world. This means that the planning which should follow the discussion about the future direction must be down to earth and concerned with things which can actually be done. It involves looking at the problems standing in the way of making the vision reality as well as looking at the opportunities and the aspects of school life which are supportive.

It is also important to recognise that work on vision is not a once-for-all activity. The vision you start by developing needs to be revisited at intervals so that it can be updated in the light of current circumstances and changed to meet the development that has taken place since the work started.

QUESTIONS FOR CONSIDERATION

1 What is the culture of this school? What do people believe about education and about children and the way they learn? What is my evidence for this?

2 In what ways will the existing culture of the school support my work? In what ways does it need to be changed or developed?

3 How do the staff generally deal with problems, whether these are individual or collective?

4 Do people trust and support each other?

5 Do staff work together to plan the way forward?

6 Do they do this in my subject?

7 How do people react to new ideas? Are they prepared to try things out?

8 What does the head teacher's vision for the school appear to be?

9 How am I going to set about developing a vision for the teaching of my subject?

10 What is my vision for working with colleagues in developing work in my subject?

CHAPTER 4

Policies and schemes of work

As a subject leader you will be responsible for the policies and schemes of work for your subject. There may already be a policy for the subject and a scheme of work in existence, but you may want to modify these. If either or both are non-existent you will need to see about providing them.

The school may already have a policy for teaching and learning which will cover practice in your subject, although you may want to provide some guidelines about how this policy provides for the subject.

Bell and Ritchie suggest that the purpose of having a school teaching and learning policy is that it will:

- lead to everyone having a clear picture of the teaching and learning strategies employed throughout the school;
- help to build up teams working towards common, agreed goals;
- develop an appreciation of the extent to which individual actions help or hinder consistency and continuity of the learning process;
- increase the level of commitment and ownership of the decisions and the necessary actions to implement them;
- provide opportunities for different points of view to be expressed and misunderstandings to be resolved at an early stage;
- reinforce the collective responsibility for the implementation of agreed actions and decisions. (1999:65, 66)

They also suggest that having such a policy is valuable for introducing new teachers to the school's practices and provides continuity both within subject areas and across subjects.

West supports the idea of a general learning and teaching policy on the grounds that:

> As they participate in learning, pupils engage in investigative work, problem solving, hypothesising, trialling, testing and exploring, communicating and so on; they acquire new concepts and extend existing conceptual frameworks, and they practise new skills and engage in their work through a mixed economy of individual, group and whole-class activities. The differences between subjects lie in the nature of evidence that is cited in the different subjects and the tests for truth which are applied in the course of learning. (1998:29)

It may be helpful when considering how to set about producing a subject policy to look at any policies produced by other subjects. It would also be wise to discuss your plans for producing or updating the subject policy with your head teacher who may want to contribute ideas to it or to suggest that particular approaches to learning are stressed.

A policy, whether it is a subject-specific policy or a more general teaching and learning policy, needs the following elements:

1. An introductory statement of the rationale of the subject, what is involved in teaching it and its role in the education of children or, in the case of a teaching and learning policy, a more general statement about the school's view of teaching and learning.
2. A brief statement about aims, including desirable long-term outcomes. This statement should include reference to the National Curriculum.
3. A more detailed statement about the objectives stemming from the aims, again relating to the National Curriculum.
4. A description of desirable teaching approaches. This might stress the need for first-hand experience and investigative work, make suggestions for group work, emphasise the need for differentiation to cater for children of all abilities, note the importance of progression and continuity and cross-curricular links and suggest ways of using ICT. In a subject policy there should be details about desirable approaches in that subject, e.g. practical work in science and design and technology, field work in geography and history.
5. Guidance on assessment and record-keeping, with suggestions about the way in which children's progress might be recorded and level assessments made. This might also include a reference to the school's assessment policy.
6. Guidance on providing for children with special educational needs and for children with exceptional ability.
7. A reference to the resources available for the subject and the system for accessing them. There should also be a separate document about resources in most subjects to which this policy may refer.
8. A statement about safety in subjects where this is relevant.
9. Suggestions about links with other subjects.

A policy should be dated and be as brief as is compatible with covering the necessary ground. It should be reviewed at regular intervals to see that it is still relevant.

It is desirable for the production or the revision of a subject policy to be the outcome of group discussion. The headings given above may be useful in setting the agenda for such a meeting, during which teachers and perhaps some classroom assistants may offer suggestions about things they would like to see included. A school policy for teaching and learning should also be widely discussed, and where such a document exists it may be necessary to provide additional advice about teaching in the subject to be used alongside it.

CASE STUDY

Jonathan had just been appointed as subject leader for design and technology. He had been teaching for a number of years and as a very practical person had been enthusiastic about teaching this subject for some time. He was conscious that there was a lack of continuity in the work that was currently being done and wanted to develop a new scheme of work which would offer guidance to teachers of all year groups as they moved through the school.

He started by asking everyone to let him have details of the work they had covered in the past year. This gave him a picture of what had been happening and he combined all the information to make a statement that everyone could see and discuss. He found some overlap and some omissions in the reports which his colleagues had produced and he was able to pinpoint areas where discussion was needed to sort out what should be done at different stages.

He then went on to talk with staff about his findings in the endeavour to get some agreement about the skills, knowledge and concepts which should be taught and learned in each year. The staff discussed the report that Jonathan had prepared and came to an agreement about the topics which should be covered each year, the kinds of records they would keep and the resources which they would need. This became the basis of a revised scheme of work.

A scheme of work needs to include the following:

1. A statement of the key areas of the National Curriculum being covered by the scheme.
2. A statement of learning objectives including skills, knowledge, concepts or underlying ideas and suggestions about the way in which the content might be organised over the course of the year, giving possible time allocations to the different topics and any options within the scheme from which teachers can select. This may be the place for stating the kinds of attitudes to the subject that teachers should be trying to develop in children.
3. A statement of the kinds of teaching and learning methods and activities which might be provided, including the use of ICT and the provision for differentiation by ability.
4. A statement about the way in which the learning material might be

structured – is it, for example, to be divided into modules or themes? How are these to be timed?

5. Information about the resources available for the teaching of the subject and how to access them.

6. A statement about the kind of learning outcomes and assessments which might be expected, how these will be evaluated, the criteria which may be used and the types of record which should be kept.

7. Information about links with other areas of curriculum such as literacy, numeracy and ICT.

8. A statement about any health and safety elements likely to arise in teaching the subject.

As subject leader you may need to provide further documentation to support the policy and scheme of work. You may want to offer further suggestions about ways of working, such as cooperative group work or the use of ICT. You may also want to provide information about the resources available at school level and how to access them. The practical subjects such as design and technology, science, art and design, music and physical education may need particular advice either as part of the scheme of work or as a separate document.

QUESTIONS FOR CONSIDERATION

1 Is there a school teaching and learning policy or do I need to provide a subject policy?

2 What do I feel are the essential elements in teaching my subject?

3 What teaching and learning strategies do I want to see colleagues using in my subject? What part should ICT play?

4 Does the scheme we have worked out provide for continuity and progression?

5 Does the scheme support teachers in differentiating work for children of different abilities?

6 How does the policy and scheme of work in my subject relate to other subject policies and schemes of work? Is there encouragement for cross-curricular work?

7 Are we agreed on the kinds of records which we will keep for work in this subject?

8 Do colleagues know of the resources available for teaching this subject and how to access them?

CHAPTER 5

Development planning

An important aspect of the subject leader role is planning for development. Schools need to be concerned with continuous improvement and this means that development planning should be an ongoing activity, with plans being developed and agreed annually.

The National Standards for Subject Leaders suggest that

subject leaders should establish, with the involvement of relevant staff, short, medium and long-term plans for the development and resourcing of the subject which:

- contribute to whole-school aims, policies and practices, including those in relation to behaviour, discipline, bullying and racial harassment;
- are based on a range of comparative information and evidence, including that in relation to the attainment of pupils;
- identify realistic and challenging targets for improvement in the subject;
- are understood by all those involved in putting the plans into practice;
- are clear about the action to be taken, timescales and criteria for success. (Teacher Training Agency 1998:10)

All schools must have a school development plan setting out long- and medium-term strategic plans. The subject development plan is a further development of the school plan, feeding into it and developing further from it. Hargreaves and Hopkins suggest that there are eight main advantages to development planning:

1. A development plan focuses on the aims of education, especially the learning and achievement, broadly defined, of all pupils.
2. A development plan provides a comprehensive and coordinated approach to all aspects of planning, one which covers curriculum and assessment, teaching, management and organisation, finance and resources.
3. The development plan captures the long-term vision for the school within which manageable short-term goals are set. The priorities contained in the plan represent the school's translation of policy into its agenda for action.
4. A development plan helps to relieve the stress on teachers caused by the pace of change. Teachers come to exercise greater control over change rather than feel controlled by it.

5. The achievements of teachers in promoting innovation and change receive wider recognition, so that their confidence rises.
6. The quality of staff development improves. In-service training and appraisal help the school to work more effectively and help teachers acquire new knowledge and skills as part of their professional development.
7. The partnership between the teaching staff and the governing body is strengthened.
8. The task of reporting on the work of the school is made easier.
(1991:6, 7)

These points refer to the school development plan but the advantages listed also apply to a good subject development plan.

Planning for the subject starts with the vision. It was suggested in Chapter 3 that staff should try to envisage what the desirable state of the subject might be in two or three years' time. Development planning is the next step from creating a vision statement. The vision statement may be rather vague and the planning process has to translate it into specific aims and objectives and a route to achieving them.

Development planning starts with an audit of the current state of things. If you have recently been appointed to your post you will have already started to do this. If you have been in post for some time you may need to make a new audit as a starting point for planning. An audit certainly involves discussion with colleagues and your head teacher about what they think needs further development. It may involve some monitoring of what is already happening in classrooms, perhaps by observation, but also by looking at children's work and seeing what is being currently achieved and by talking to staff. You may also learn by talking with children about their work and you may want to review the resources available for the subject and consider how they need to be developed and used more profitably.

One form of analysis which it may be profitable to undertake at this stage is known as a SWOT analysis – a review of the strengths and weaknesses of the present situation and the opportunities and threats which a change would present. This will give you a picture of the task before you and help you to consider the problems you may encounter.

Once you have reviewed the current situation you need to go back to your vision statement and see how this fits with the findings of the audit. Bell and Ritchie suggest that you may like to ask yourself the following questions and discuss them with your colleagues:

- What is your concern? What do you want to improve?
- What specific aspect of the concern do you want to address?
- What ideas do you have about how to improve the situation?
- What are realistic goals?
- What precise action are you going to take?
- Who do you hope will support you? What kind of support do you need?
- What evidence will you collect to show that you have able to improve the situation?
- When and how will you evaluate progress? (1999:44)

You also need to consider the time and resources available for the teaching of the subject in each year group, including the provision for ICT.

You first need to set out the broad aims for your planning and then turn the aims into goals in terms which as far as possible are specific and measurable. For example, in geography you may want at some stage to specify that all pupils will be able to interpret scale on a map; that they know, for example, that a centimetre on the map represents a mile in the countryside represented. In design and technology you may want to specify that all pupils are able to use certain tools safely. Your objectives may be intellectual ones as in the geography goals given above, or physical as in the goal for technology. You also need to give a period within which such skills and knowledge will be achieved and consider how their achievement will be assessed. Not all your objectives will be as specific as this but you need to make them as specific as possible. Discussion with colleagues will help you to make the statements realistic. You also need to think about the criteria by which you and your colleagues will assess the success of their work. This can be very helpful in making the objectives specific.

You may also have some aims which are attitudinal, such as endeavouring to increase children's enthusiasm for reading, and although it is more difficult to measure the success of such aims you need to try to find ways of assessing how far they have been achieved. You might, for example, check on the number of books which have been borrowed from the library.

When you have a first draft of the plan drawn up you need to consider the following:

- What should be the starting date for the implementation of the plan?
- How does the plan apply to each year group? Are there any gaps?
- Does the plan meet the statutory requirements of the National Curriculum?
- What elements in this plan should be part of the School Development Plan?

- Which of the objectives listed are priorities?
- Are there any areas which overlap with work in other subjects?
- What resources will teachers need? How should these be organised?
- What support or professional development opportunities will teachers need?
- What records of work should teachers keep?
- Are there any implications for support staff?
- When and how will the effect of the plan be evaluated?
- What will be the success criteria by which the work undertaken will be judged?
- How should the completed plan be introduced to colleagues?

It may be a good idea to undertake what is known as Force Field Analysis, a system devised by Kurt Lewin (1938). This involves considering the positive forces which will help you to implement your plan and the negative forces which will work against you. Positive forces might be support from the head teacher, good resources for the subject and a certain amount of enthusiasm from some staff. Negative forces might be a lack of enthusiasm from a small minority of colleagues, a general dislike of change and pressure on time for everyone concerned. The task is then to consider how to make the most of the supporting forces and how to minimise the negative ones. Jackson suggests looking at negative forces as obstacles and to consider whether any of the following approaches to each particular obstacle might work: 'overcome it, go round it, remove it, demolish it, neutralise it, prove it to be illusory, turn it to advantage, buy it off, alter, find its weakest point, wait for it to go away' (1975).

CASE STUDY

Rosemary was subject leader for history in a two-form entry junior school. She worked with colleagues to make a development plan for the next year which covered each year group and they set about putting it into action. However, she felt some concern for the pressure on teachers in turning the development plan into plans for each lesson, since a good deal of the material they had agreed to include involved new thinking. She therefore started to think of ways in which they could share planning and make it less arduous for individuals.

She arranged with the head teacher that the morning of the next in-service day could be devoted to planning for history. She arranged for one of the teachers from each year group, including herself, to make a presentation describing the plan for a lesson which had gone particularly well, with the idea that this plan could be used by the other teacher in the year group. She then suggested that if everyone agreed to put lesson plans on the computer these could be accessed by all and would save time in that the plans would simply need customising for the class in question rather than planning from scratch. It would be a time-consuming job in the first instance but would save them a great deal of time in the long run.

They all agreed that this would be a good idea and they set about making an outline for planning which would be common to all the plans. The outline started with the aims and objectives of the lesson, described starter activities or presentation, listed group and individual work, and a final plenary. Resources were also listed.

It was agreed that since there were two classes in each year group, each pair of teachers would undertake the planning of half the lessons in their section of the scheme of work and set them out as plans which someone else could work from.

When the plan is finally agreed it may be a good idea to put it onto the computer so that people can access it whenever they need to. You may need to offer help to some colleagues for some aspects of the plan, perhaps sharing a lesson with them if it can be timetabled or giving a demonstration lesson on a particular topic. You will need to check on progress with it from time to time, asking colleagues how their plans are going and looking at children's work, or perhaps holding a meeting to discuss progress. You need to look for changes in practice in particular and assess how each of the objectives in the plan has worked out in practice. It may be a good idea to ask each teacher to report on his or her success in achieving each of the objectives.

QUESTIONS FOR CONSIDERATION

1 What do I need to do by way of auditing existing practice?

2 Is there anything in the school development plan which will affect the subject development plan?

3 How should I set about involving colleagues in the development plan?

4 Has the subject development plan any implications for other subject areas?

5 Has the plan any implications for resources?

6 What should be the success criteria for the different elements of the plan?

7 How should we evaluate progress with the plan?

CHAPTER 6

Leading the team

Most primary school staffs see themselves as a team because, unlike secondary schools, numbers of staff are small enough for people to know each other well. It is important that the staff work together as a group and develop collegiality if the school is to work well. While the head teacher is the overall leader of the staff, almost every teacher, at some time, will be in a leadership role. As a subject leader you will have opportunities to lead the staff in relation to work in your subject.

The leadership role

Bastide gives the following description of the subject coordinator role:

> The role of any subject coordinator, whatever the subject is, is largely about influencing other people. The ideal coordinator is an enthusiastic model to colleagues; is knowledgeable about the curriculum concerned; keeps up to date with developments at a local and national level; listens to and acknowledges colleagues' concerns; is prepared to start from the point colleagues are at and to work from these; is prepared to work collaboratively with colleagues and offer support where it is needed; to be a critical friend (both supporting and challenging) and above all to have a vision for the subject in the school. (1999:7)

The National Standards for Subject Leaders suggest that where other staff teach or support the subject, subject leaders should be able to:

1. secure commitment to a clear aim and direction for the subject;
2. prioritise, plan and organise;
3. work as part of a team;
4. deal sensitively with people, recognise individual needs and take account of these in securing a consistent team approach to raising achievement in the subject;
5. acknowledge and use the experience, expertise and contribution of others;
6. set standards and provide a role model for pupils and other staff, in the teaching and learning of the subject;
7. devolve responsibilities and delegate tasks, as appropriate;
8. seek advice and support when necessary. (Teacher Training Agency 1998:7)

The leadership role for subject leaders may be less easy than some other leadership roles, and since in most schools almost everyone will need to lead a subject, the role may not attract additional salary. You may also be fairly junior in terms of experience and may yet be expected to lead the work of teachers who are older and much more experienced than you are. On the other hand, you will have been asked to undertake this role because you have knowledge and skill in your subject, and you can draw confidence from this.

One of the most obvious ways in which you will be able to demonstrate leadership of your subject will be in the teaching of the subject in your own class. Your skill in the classroom will help your colleagues to have confidence in your leadership.

As a good subject team leader you should be knowledgeable about your subject area, first from initial study and training and then from keeping up to date with developments by reading relevant books and papers and taking part in in-service courses. You should be able to keep colleagues informed about developments in the subject area.

You should have your own vision of good teaching in the subject area and work with colleagues through discussion to develop a common vision which is acceptable to them all and can provide broad aims for their work. The vision should be revisited from time to time to keep it up to date and an appropriate basis for setting goals and targets.

You need to be seen to work hard, effectively and efficiently, providing a good role model for colleagues in both your classroom teaching and in the leadership role, running effective meetings and dealing with day-to-day problems and difficulties, organising resources so that they are easily available to colleagues and dealing with necessary paperwork, and ensuring that the subject policies and schemes of work are up to date and workable.

You need to be a good communicator. Communication is the sharing of thoughts, feelings and experiences. Sharing means finding out how others think and feel as well as telling them your thoughts and giving them information. Some of this exchange of communication will be individual as you talk with colleagues at intervals during the school day and some of it will be information exchanged during meetings. Think out carefully the messages you want to give to meetings. Consider the views of those who will be on the receiving end of the communication and provide an opportunity for feedback to give you an idea of whether the message has been understood and accepted. Part of communication is the ability to listen. Are you a good listener? It is very easy to listen with half an ear and with your mind on what you want to say next.

It is very important to be supportive of other people, ready to help them with problems, listening to them and taking their views seriously and showing that you value their contributions. You should make a point of noticing their work and thanking them for what they offer to the staff group. You also need to be concerned to develop their confidence and self-esteem, particularly in the case of newly qualified teachers or teachers who feel uncertain about the best way to work in your subject. They may need reassuring that they are making progress and doing the right thing. If they are not working well you need to look out for any aspect of what they are doing which you can praise and encourage before going on to explain how to avoid the mistakes they are making.

A good subject leader has good interpersonal skills and communicates effectively. You need to keep people informed about what is happening and give them opportunities to comment on developments. You need to be able to run meetings efficiently so that people feel that they are time well spent, where they can express their views and be part of the decision-making process.

You need to develop the skill of analysing situations in order to solve problems. This involves collecting information about the problem, defining it clearly, generating ideas about how to proceed, preferably in consultation with other people and then selecting a way forward, putting the solution into practice and evaluating the result. This is not easy and some problems may remain intractable or not within your sphere of influence to solve. The task is to find a way through which is the best you can manage in the circumstances.

You need to show that you are willing to take responsibility and take decisions when necessary after consulting people. Sometimes there will be differences of opinion about the best way forward and you may not be able to get everyone to agree. If you have explored the territory fully with colleagues and been unable to get full agreement you may need to make a firm decision yourself and help those who disagree to come to terms with it.

You need to ensure that everyone is aware of the resources in the school for use in your subject and knows how to access them when they are needed. You need to keep resources under review so that you are in a position to request new or additional resources when finance is available. You also need to be knowledgeable about what ICT may have to offer in your subject.

You cannot help colleagues to a full extent unless you are aware of what they are doing in the classroom. There will not be many opportunities to observe others in action but you can learn a good deal from talking to people informally and looking at children's work and classroom displays. You may also be part of a scheme to exchange classes with other teachers from time to time so that you can judge how work is going in your partner's class in your subject while he or she makes judgements about how your class is doing in the subject he or she leads.

Leading the team

In most schools the team you lead from time to time will be the whole staff team and it will already have characteristics as a team which will affect the way you can work with its members. Whatever the way other teachers work with the staff team you need to develop your own leadership style and help colleagues to be effective team members when you are in the leadership role.

Fleming and Amesbury suggest that a team is characterised by:

- members sharing vision;
- members being interdependent;
- members knowing what the teams goals are;
- members understanding what their unique contribution to achieving the goals is;
- members communicating openly;
- members supporting and trusting each other;
- healthy debate between members;
- relaxed but purposeful relationships. (2001:70)

They go on to speak of the open communication climate characteristic of effective teams:

- Communication encourages and values everyone regardless of status.
- Communication shows empathy and understanding.
- Feedback and debate are encouraged.
- There is a focus on collective problem-solving.
- Statements are informative, not evaluative.
- Error is recognised and minimised.
- There are no hidden messages.

You will be in a leadership role with the staff team for a specific set of purposes – the development of the teaching and learning of your subject. You need to be clear about the outcomes you expect from the work of the team and ensure that everyone shares your expectations. What do you hope to achieve as a group? How will you evaluate this achievement? How will you know if the team is being successful?

An effective teacher team:

- has clear procedures for meetings and for arriving at decisions and tackling problems;
- has learning as a clear priority – both the learning of children and that of the team members;
- listens actively to the ideas and suggestions of its members and gives them full consideration;
- discusses and shares its objectives, recognising the values held by its members and working out ways of dealing with any differences in views;
- translates objectives into agreed tasks;
- has open communication and a climate of support in which team members talk about their work and share problems and seek solutions together;
- reviews the progress of work in the subject at regular intervals;
- endeavours to make conflict constructive by discussing differences openly and recognising people's feelings about an issue.

Running a meeting

As subject leader, you will from time to time have the opportunity to chair a staff meeting to discuss issues in your subject. It is important to think clearly in advance about the purpose of the meeting you plan and the objectives you hope to achieve from it. It may be to deal with certain aspects of administration, to discuss new ideas and developments, to evaluate progress, to solve problems or decide policy.

You need to prepare well for such a meeting, sending out an agenda in good time which makes clear the main purposes of the meeting and what you hope will be the outcome. It is a good idea to list the purpose of each item on the agenda, giving the outcome you hope will stem from it. For some items you may be hoping to get a decision. For others you may simply want to know what people think or you may want to give information. Try to arrange the agenda so that some time is spent on exchanging information about teaching methods and strategies. You may also want to send out any papers giving information about topics to be discussed at the meeting, so that colleagues can read them in advance and be ready to discuss them.

It is a good discipline and helpful to colleagues to give a finishing time for the meeting, which means you must move the meeting along to achieve it. It can also be helpful to note on your copy of the agenda how long you expect each item to take. This helps you to be disciplined in the amount of time you allow for discussion.

In preparing for the meeting you need to consider whether there any resources that will be needed. Do you need an overhead projector or flip-chart? Do you need a computer for a PowerPoint presentation? Do you want to show a tape? Are there any documents which people will need? You also need to decide who you will ask to take notes and produce the minutes. You need to do this well in advance so that the person concerned can be briefed. It may be a good idea to rotate this task so that no particular person has too much to do. The minutes should include the following:

- the time and date of the meeting;
- a list of those present, including apologies for absence;
- a brief statement of the items discussed, the conclusions reached, the decisions made and the actions agreed;
- the names of those responsible for actions.

You also need to think through in advance how you are going to introduce the various agenda items. You may want to ask other people to introduce some of them and, if this is the case, it is a good idea to brief people in advance so that they are ready. Other items you may decide to introduce yourself and it is a good idea to think out beforehand what you will say, particularly if the item is likely to be controversial. Think about possible arguments and counter arguments so that you are ready to deal with them and if necessary sound out people who may be concerned before the meeting about anything likely to cause a problem.

The venue for a meeting makes a difference to how it goes. The best set-up for a group meeting is to sit in a circle so that everyone can see and hear everyone else. Try to avoid seating people against the light, as this is distracting, particularly if the person chairing the meeting has his or her back to the light so that other people need to look into the light when they speak to him or her. Comfort is also important. A meeting where everyone is seated on infant-sized chairs or where the temperature is too hot or too cold is likely to be affected by people's discomfort and they will want to get to the end of the meeting as quickly as possible. There is something to be said for meeting in different people's classrooms in turn and using the occasion to look at work there.

Make sure that you start the meeting at the time given on the agenda. If you get into the habit of starting late, people may anticipate this and turn up late. If there are minutes from a previous meeting you need to start by considering what action has been taken on the points listed there. It is a good idea to open the main part of the meeting by reminding people of its purpose and you need to return to this at intervals if the discussion strays too far from your intentions.

Once an item has been introduced you need to encourage people to give their views about it. You need to be alert to people wanting to contribute. Very often a person will sit forward and look as if he or she wants to say something and your task is to see that everyone who wants to contribute actually does so, at the same time ensuring that particular individuals do not dominate the discussion. The way you receive contributions will determine the extent to which people feel they can contribute. If people feel that you are welcoming and positive about what they have to say they will be more ready to give their views. It can be useful when there is a particularly difficult issue under discussion to get the group to discuss it in pairs before discussing it as a whole group. The pairs can then report back to the full meeting. This gives everyone a chance to think through what is being discussed and may give rise to a wider variety of ideas than whole-group discussion.

Another important aspect of running a meeting is awareness of body language. You will be sending messages to your colleagues by the way you smile at them and look accepting of their contributions. Perhaps you will look at your watch at some stage, conveying that you are concerned about time and perhaps giving a hint that some people are going on for too long. You will also be reading the body language of others. One of the team looking at her watch may signal that she is getting bored and wishes you would get on with it. People show their feelings facially and they often start to fidget when they are not happy with what is being said, and the fidgeting will probably be exaggerated if the person concerned is feeling very strongly. Much of our understanding of body language is unconscious but if you are aware of what is going on, observation of how people sit and move is informative.

You may help the discussion to move along by judicious questioning including questions which encourage people to describe how they feel about a proposal. A question like, 'Can you tell us a bit more about that?' or 'How do people feel about that idea?' may open out discussion and encourage people to contribute. It is important to be sensitive to the way people may react if others are critical of their ideas. Such criticism may be taken as a personal attack and you need to be ready to offer support to the person being criticised. You also need to be ready to cope with such criticisms applied to you, asking for further information about why the criticism is being made and how the person making it would like things to be different, rather than becoming defensive. It may be a good opportunity for learning!

Once discussion is under way your task is first of all to be an active listener, really concentrating on what people are saying rather than letting your thoughts wander. You then need to draw the discussion points together for the group, summarising from time to time the points that have been raised and moving the group on if it seems that people have said all they wish to say about a particular issue. It may be necessary to draw a conclusion from a part of the discussion or agree action on someone's part, so that the person taking the minutes can record this. Try to keep your objectives for the meeting in mind as the discussion proceeds so that you can get the discussion back on track if it goes off course.

At the end of the meeting you need to see if there are any other points that people want to make and then summarise the points that have been agreed and take note of any decisions that have been deferred to the next meeting. You then need to go over the actions that have been agreed so that each person knows what he or she has to do. If time allows, you may also like to ask colleagues how they feel the meeting went as part of your evaluation of it.

You may find it helpful during a meeting to use an overhead projector or a flip-chart to record ideas as they are suggested. They can be written as a list or, if the topic lends itself, as a concept map with a central idea written in the middle of the sheet, and ideas as they are suggested linked to it by lines and arrows. This sort of material can then form part of the record of the meeting, either as part of the minutes or as a separate record of ideas that have been agreed.

In the course of the meeting you may have to deal with various difficulties. There may be someone who tries to dominate the meeting, contributing at length when other people want to get their contribution in. You need to cut such a person short politely when he or she has had a fair hearing, saying something like, 'Thank you, Martin, that's a very interesting point. Perhaps other people want to comment on it now.' Another problem is the person who says nothing. In this case you may need to address the person individually during the meeting and ask for an opinion, or perhaps seek him or her out after the meeting to ask whether there was any reason why he or she did not want to contribute.

After the meeting it is a good idea to think back over what happened and reflect critically on how well it went. Did the meeting achieve the objectives with which you started out? Were people given enough information in advance? Was the environment conducive to a good meeting? How did the discussion go? What conclusions were reached? Were you happy about the decisions made? Were there any problems for you as chair of the meeting? Did anyone talk too much or too little? What changes would you make at the next meeting? You will also want to liaise with the minute-taker to see that the minutes are an accurate reflection of what happened.

CASE STUDY

Richard and Mary were subject leaders for mathematics and religious education respectively in a two-form entry junior school. They were both new in post although Mary had worked in the school for three years previously. Both were concerned to develop their skills in leading meetings and wanted to get feedback on how they were doing. They agreed that they would each, in turn, act as an observer at the other's subject meeting and provide some feedback on how the meeting went.

Richard had arranged a meeting to discuss the records teachers should keep of children's progress in mathematics. He particularly wanted to get people to keep records which would be of value to the next teacher when the children moved up the school. He had provided an agenda for the meeting which set out this aim so that people could think about it in advance.

Mary observed the meeting and made notes of what happened. She found that although Richard did listen to what others were suggesting, he did not make very encouraging responses to people's contributions and they tended to be a bit limited and he tended to talk too much himself as a result. However, he summed up very ably at different points in the meeting and at the end, so that people went away clear about what they were going to do.

Mary wanted to use her meeting to get some agreement on the visits to various places of worship which would be part of the programme of religious education in the coming year. This hadn't happened before and some teachers were uncertain about the idea. The agenda she provided was very brief. Richard found when he observed the meeting that she was good at getting other people to express their views and was very encouraging so that contributions came easily. She found it difficult to get people to reconcile their views about the desirability of making the visits, however, and was not good at summing up what had been said. Consequently the meeting went on a long time and finished without any real agreement.

Negotiation

You may find that there are occasions when you have to negotiate with your colleagues, perhaps about a change you would like to see introduced or a development you would like to see. Different people may have different views about what you are proposing and some may be against it. You may therefore need to do some bargaining. Fisher and Ury list four basic points for principled bargaining:

1. *People* – separate the people from the problem.
2. *Interests* – focus on interests, not positions.
3. *Options* – generate a variety of possibilities before deciding what to do.
4. *Criteria* – insist that the result is based on objective criteria. (1983:11)

They suggest that the aim is that 'participants should see themselves working side by side, attacking the problem, not each other'. They set out three possible stages for negotiation:

1. *Analysis:* Diagnose the situation, gather information, organise it and think about it. Consider people problems. Identify interests on both sides. Note possible options. Identify any criteria for decisions that have already been suggested as a basis for agreement.
2. *Planning:* Deal with the same four elements given above, generating ideas and deciding what to do. Generate additional options and criteria.
3. *Discussion:* Let people talk out their views and feelings about what is proposed. Acknowledge differences in perceptions, any feelings of frustration and anger and try to see that each side recognises how the other party feels. Then go on to generate options which are mutually advantageous.

Problem-solving in a group has the advantage that there are more ideas and proposals to consider than when one tries to solve a problem single-handed. Members of the group often stimulate each other and as a result there is more chance that someone will come up with a really good idea. After discussing the ideas put forward you can then go on to see if you can get agreement to one of them or to a combination of several ideas.

Brainstorming may be a useful activity to generate ideas to help to solve a problem. Set out some ground rules – for example, every idea should be treated positively and not criticised at the generating ideas stage. Then record all the ideas suggested in full view of everyone. Record far-fetched ideas as well as more ordinary ones, rejecting nothing. When people seem to have exhausted their ideas, start discussing the most promising ideas and look for ways of making them even better. Look for a range of possible options to discuss and take further. Look for solutions which bring the most gain to the most people. Very often a good solution will incorporate more than one of the ideas suggested. You may reach a solution fairly easily or it may be that there are differences of opinion.

The aim in a situation where people are finding it difficult to agree is to focus on the overall outcome which both sides want to achieve and try to find a way in which both sides can win, perhaps by redefining the task and providing an over-riding goal which both sides accept. Look for a second-best or alternative solution to which everyone can agree. It is usually better if you have time to go on searching for a solution than to decide an issue by vote, which may leave those whose views were not chosen feeling aggrieved and unready to carry out the action decided upon.

Dealing with conflict

Most people in leadership roles will have to deal with conflict from time to time. This is not a failure – conflict can be a positive thing if you can work through it to a solution which meets the needs of those who disagreed initially. Conflict can lead to growth and without differences of opinion the work of the team will probably stagnate. Conflict is of various types. People can disagree because they hold different beliefs and values. There can also be conflict when there is no clear line between different people's responsibilities and they have a conflict over territory. This could happen between a teacher and a classroom assistant as well as between teachers. There may also be conflict between people who just dislike each other for no particular reason.

Conflict over philosophy needs to be talked out, getting people to try to agree common goals, but if those concerned still cannot agree you may have to accept that different people work differently, while endeavouring to bring them as close to a common goal as you can. The group can learn from the different ways in which people wish to work, and the conflict can have a positive effect.

Conflict may arise because resources are limited and everyone wants the same materials. In this case you will need to arbitrate and arrange for people to take turns, at the same time seeing if it is possible to increase the resources to meet people's needs. You need to be open about his and try to be as fair as possible.

Conflict over territory can often be resolved by helping each person to define his or her responsibilities clearly and sorting out where one person's responsibility ends and another person's begins. It often helps to generate a variety of possible ways forward before arriving at a decision.

When conflict occurs in a meeting it is first of all important for everyone to have an opportunity to put their point of view. If the views expressed seem irreconcilable it is often a good idea to leave the controversial topic for a time and discuss something else and then return to the topic later in the meeting. Sometimes people revise their views when this happens and find it easier to come to some agreement.

Woodcock warns of the problems of destructive conflict:

> Destructive conflict, which defeats cooperation, can occur when an individual's carefully built images are threatened, when personalities obtrude, when conflict is expected and the expectation becomes self-fulfilling, or when two parties are arguing about different things without realising it. (1979:192)

As team leader you need to be alert to this kind of conflict and do your best to support anyone who seems to be under attack.

One strategy is to turn the conflict into fruitful competition. Where two people are in conflict about how to do something, it may be possible to agree on the desired outcome and then let both parties set about achieving it in the way they favour. If this is reviewed later there may be useful learning for everyone.

Fisher and Ury suggest that in handling conflict in a group the following may help:

- separate people from problems;
- focus on people's interests rather than on positions rigidly held;
- establish precise goals at the onset of discussion;
- work together to invent creative solutions that will satisfy the interests of all parties. (1983)

Cawood and Gibbon (1981) contrast mature and immature groups. In mature groups people listen attentively to each other and express their views openly and freely. They deal with controversial issues without becoming antagonistic. They seek to understand before expressing opinions and try to find aspects of any issue with which they can agree. They try to use the talents of all the group members. In immature groups these things are less likely to happen.

Kemp and Nathan list the following comments made by teachers about good team leaders:

- She really does listen to what we have to say.
- He works hard and expects the same from us.
- She is good about thanking you for what you do – it's always nice to feel appreciated for things you have done really well.
- If she feels you are not doing something as well as you should, then she says so – she's firm but fair.
- He's not afraid to make difficult decisions.
- There's no doubt who is the leader of the team, but we are all made to feel that we are contributing. (1989:114)

QUESTIONS FOR CONSIDERATION

1 What are my strengths as a team leader?

2 Am I keeping up to date with developments in my subject?

3 How would I describe good teaching in my subject?

4 How would colleagues describe my skill as a communicator?

5 What do I do to help colleagues develop their self-esteem?

6 Do people give their views freely at subject meetings?

7 How good am I at helping the staff group solve problems?

8 How well do I deal with conflict?

CHAPTER 7

Providing for professional development

As a subject leader, it is your task to help your colleagues to develop professionally in the teaching of your subject. There are many ways in which you can do this, some of them informal opportunities occurring in the course of daily work which you can use and others which are carefully planned opportunities for teacher learning.

Professional development is a continuing need for all teachers. It should be part of the school culture. Teachers need to be constantly searching for the best ways of enabling children to learn, keeping pace with change, developing their knowledge and developing as people. The best teachers are enthusiastic learners who do all they can to help the children they teach to become enthusiastic learners too. A school will have a culture about teacher learning which may support it or be antagonistic to the idea. As subject leader you need to encourage teacher learning. Your school probably has someone with responsibility for professional development and you need to work with him or her to ensure development and learning in your subject. You may also want a slot in the programme of an Inset day.

Your ideas about professional development will be related to the vision you have developed for the teaching of your subject and to ideas you may have about the way in which you would like to see the teaching change and develop. It may be helpful to try to set out your aims for professional development so that you have a clear idea of what you are aiming to do which guides you in planning a programme which includes both informal and formal elements for teacher learning.

An overall goal for work in your subject is to raise expectations and so to raise levels of performance. Professional development of staff is a step towards such a goal. Possible goals for the professional development of colleagues may include the following:

- increasing teachers' subject knowledge;
- developing planning ability in the subject;
- developing relevant teaching skills in the subject, including the use of ICT;
- developing appropriate organisational skills where these are relevant.

You also need to consider what development opportunities may be needed by support staff. Learning support assistants may need help in providing for children learning your subject.

In planning for the professional development of colleagues you need to take into account what is known about the way adults learn best. Research suggests that adults need opportunities that involve reflection, analysis and critical examination. They benefit from a situation where there is mutual helpfulness and peer support. They like to be actively involved in the learning process and to pace their own learning. They like practical situations which they can apply to their classroom practice. Macbeath and Myers suggest that people learn when there is:

- a reason or a stimulus to learn;
- a climate which encourages exploration and risk-taking;
- models to observe and learn from;
- opportunities to test out what is being learned;
- the possibility of success;
- opportunities to learn from mistakes;
- support and encouragement;
- feedback about success and progress;
- self-belief. (1999:38)

It is helpful in planning professional development opportunities to make an audit of what development people feel they need. You may do this by talking to colleagues individually or collectively or by asking them to complete a questionnaire specifying their needs as they see them. You also need to consider the development needs of which people are unaware. You will get an idea of this from visiting classrooms and talking to individuals. The school may have a professional development committee which does this in fairly general terms which will provide a background for a more specific audit of subject needs. You also need to look at professional development needs from the point of view of the children. What do they need in your subject? When you have analysed needs you then need to look at which of the expressed needs are priorities. You can then go on to consider how they can be met.

Part of your task as subject leader is to encourage people to reflect on their work and this should be part of any professional development activity you plan. You may do this by asking questions about it and by providing an example by demonstrating that you reflect on what you do yourself. Reflection is helped by feedback and you need to look for ways in which teachers can get feedback on what they do, both from colleagues and children. You should also be concerned to support and perhaps raise the self-esteem of your colleagues so that they work with confidence.

You can provide for the professional development of your colleagues as a formal part of the school's in-service programme or you can create and use opportunities which occur. The following ideas may be useful.

Action research

Action research is dealt with in detail in Chapter 16. It is a valuable way of enabling teachers to learn. It involves the teacher in identifying a particular problem that he or she wants to investigate and setting up an experimental lesson designed to meet the problem.

Coaching

A newly qualified or inexperienced teacher may benefit from some coaching in teaching your subject. This might start with a discussion of the aspects of teaching which the teacher concerned is keen to improve. You then go on to talk about possible ways of achieving improvement and perhaps demonstrate them by teaching either your class or that of the teacher concerned. The lesson is discussed and important points brought out. The teacher then tries something similar in his or her own class, with you observing and providing feedback. The only problem about this approach is finding time for you to work together.

Comparing notes about the outcomes of a particular lesson

A group of teachers can agree to teach a particular topic in an agreed way and keep a note of what happens. The notes can then be shared and discussed.

Developing a study group

A group of teachers may come together to plan a development such as a method of recording children's progress in the subject. In the course of discussion those concerned will develop their ideas as well as achieving the task of creating a form of record which they can all use.

Evaluating outcomes of a change or development

All changes and developments should be evaluated to see whether they have a positive result. The evaluation should be planned at the development stage so that evidence can be collected as the the work proceeds. A small group of teachers can then look at the evidence and report on it to the wider staff group. Everyone should learn from this exercise.

Getting feedback from children

It is often helpful to talk with children about what they have enjoyed and what they feel they have learned from a particular lesson or group of lessons, and teachers can be encouraged to do this. With older children a questionnaire can be used asking questions about what has been enjoyable and what disliked, what they feel has been the best way of learning for them – group work, individual work, teacher presentation, work with a computer, and so on. It can be useful to do this for a particular lesson which has also been observed by someone else. This is called triangulation and gives the teacher three views of what happened – his or her own, the observer's and the children's.

Getting teachers to support each other

You may find a situation where one teacher is working well and could help another who is finding difficulties. This may be particularly relevant where newly qualified teachers are concerned. A newly qualified teacher may welcome help from a more experienced colleague and you may not have time to help yourself if your school is a large one. There is much to be said for trying to establish a climate where it is normal for people to help each other.

Giving a talk to a group

Where a teacher is doing something which is likely to be of interest to others, he or she can be invited to talk to the staff group about it. The teacher concerned might also be asked to put something on paper about the work so that other people can read about it

Offering ideas and suggestions in response to enquiries

As subject leader you will often be asked for ideas by other teachers and this provides an opportunity both to help the teacher concerned learn something new and at the same time increase your awareness of that teacher's knowledge of your subject which may inform plans you make for more formal provision.

Observing each other teaching

It is very difficult for primary schoolteachers to find a time when they can see others teach, but if it can be arranged it can be a very profitable activity. If there is a general acceptance that seeing other people teach is a useful thing to do, it makes the task of monitoring other people's work much more acceptable. It will also be useful for colleagues to see you teaching your subject. Observation of teaching should always involve a preliminary discussion about what the teacher intends to do and suggestions about what would be useful feedback. An observer might, for example, study the teacher's use of questioning, or the work of particular children or any other aspect of the lesson that the teacher concerned feels would be useful. This sort of arrangement for getting feedback will be particularly useful if you invite people to see you teach, since it gets across the message that you too are wanting to learn and improve. Hewton quotes a teacher who had been anxious at the possibility of having her teaching observed who later describes the value of peer observation. 'But as the weeks went by I realised that I was receiving constructive advice as well as compliments on my work. By the sixth session I was asking the observer to comment on certain aspects of my teaching where I felt I could do with advice' (1987:22).

Personal reading and study

You can set an example of reading with reference to your subject as widely as time allows. This puts you in a position to suggest possible reading for other people. You may find it useful to photocopy extracts from your own reading for your colleagues since they will have limited time to read more widely.

Providing opportunities for sharing ideas

It can be very helpful to take a particular topic for a meeting and ask each teacher to talk briefly about how he or she sets about teaching it. It is useful to make a record of the ideas put forward for later circulation to all members.

Providing opportunities for visits to see other people's classroom displays

It was suggested in the last chapter that meetings might be held in different people's classrooms in turn, with the teacher concerned offering a guide to the work displayed. There is also a case for suggesting that other teachers should look at a particular display of work and talk to the teacher about it.

Reporting on a course attended or a book or article read

It is a good idea to provide opportunities for colleagues to share experiences of courses attended or reading they have done. It may also be possible, if people feel it would be helpful, for different teachers to agree to read some relevant document and report on it to the group.

Team teaching

If time can be made for it, it can be useful for you to team teach a lesson with a colleague in order to help him or her with the teaching of your subject. This will be particularly helpful to newly qualified teachers or teachers who are finding work in your subject very difficult. You plan the lesson together and decide what you will each do and then evaluate the outcomes together after the lesson.

Teacher involvement in the subject development plan

Discussion about what should be included in the year's development plan for the subject is a good learning opportunity for everyone taking part. It involves thinking about what is important in teaching the subject and consideration about what developments are desirable.

Working together to produce and share resources

Groups of teachers, such as those responsible for the same year group, may find it helpful to discuss and share the resources they are making for their own classes. A group may also identify a need for a particular resource and work together to produce it.

Setting up an exhibition of good work

It has already been suggested that teachers look at each other's classroom displays. You can also gather together good work from a number of classrooms to make an exhibition in a public space in the school, such as the entrance hall or the hall. It is a good idea to make this ongoing so that visitors to the school can see good work displayed and teachers can aim to produce work that is good enough for the display. It can also be useful to provide a display for an in-service event.

CASE STUDY

Margery was the subject leader for English in a junior school. Her head teacher raised with her the problem that the SATs results were always better for reading than for writing and asked her to do something about it. She arranged for a session at an in-service day when each teacher would describe his or her most successful practice in teaching English.

Muriel who taught Year 3 described how she asked the children to close their eyes and imagine a scene, picturing what was there, the colours they could see, the things they could hear and smell and the feel of surfaces near them. She enlarged upon this and then gave the children a chance to talk about what they had pictured before writing about it. She then encouraged them to do this as a way of writing poetry or as a starting point for describing the setting for a story.

Peter taught Year 4 and had set up a correspondence for the children in his class with the children of another junior school where his wife also taught Year 4. The children had to address their letters properly and sign off correctly. Each child had a specific penfriend to whom his or her letters were addressed. The scheme was a great success. The children were thrilled to receive letters from the other class and were very keen to write back and keen also to write correctly. The scheme had been going for a term and he hoped to turn it into e-mail correspondence once the two schools had enough computers.

Margaret taught Year 5 and had experimented with giving them writing structures. For example, she had worked with them to set out what was needed when writing a story or a report and children were then expected to follow the directions for their writing.

In Year 6 Joanna was the science coordinator and used some of the time in the literacy hour to improve writing in science. She worked out with the children how to write up an experiment and gave them practice in this genre of writing.

The teachers found these and other descriptions of approaches helpful in extending their own ideas about ways of improving writing.

Planning a more formal in-service event

Over time there should be opportunities for subject leaders of all subjects to run an in-service event for the whole staff. Such opportunities will not be frequent because of the number of subjects involved, so it is important to ensure that the opportunity is well used when your turn comes round.

It is a good idea to start by trying to formulate your aims for the event. This gives you a clear starting point. You then need information about the time likely to be available and the place where the event will be held and any budgetary limitations which may affect what you plan. Do you want to bring in an outside speaker or hire a film or videotape? Will you need display facilities? An overhead projector? Provision for a PowerPoint presentation? Will people need tables? Will you want any documentation and if so, should it be distributed before the event or on the day? If the work you plan depends upon the people concerned having certain information it may be a good idea to distribute it beforehand. If you give it out on the day it can divert people's attention from what you are saying but it may be information you want to speak to.

You next need to consider the activities you want to include and work out a programme to fit the time involved. It is important to remember that a basic element in the learning process is the need to make learning one's own by talking about it or working with what has been learned. Some part of the event should include discussion in pairs or small groups. You may want to include the following:

A presentation

There may be occasions when it is possible to involve an outside speaker during an in-service day but it is more likely that you will want to make a presentation yourself to introduce discussion about your subject.

A good starting point is to make a concept map of the ideas you want to include in your talk, joining related ideas by arrows. You can then put the ideas into some sort of order. While it is important to plan carefully what you intend to say and to keep it relatively brief, it is not a good idea to write out your contribution and read it to your colleagues. A useful way of planning is to take your concept map points and turn them into a series of points, perhaps on an overhead projector transparency which you can show and talk about, or you can use a computer to project such statements. This has the advantage that you can copy the list and distribute it after the talk as a record. If you don't want to do this then it is a good idea to make notes on a series of cards which you can work through as you talk. Make a time plan for what you want to say so that you can keep within the time available.

Plan out the way you intend to begin your talk in some detail. It is often a good idea to begin with a story or anecdote which illustrates something you want to get across, and illustrations of this kind are useful in the body of the talk and make it more interesting. Check at an early stage that everyone can hear you. Make eye contact with different members of your audience as you speak – this will give you information about how well they are attending and gives the impression that you are speaking to individuals. Don't move about too much and try to avoid repeated mannerisms of speech or movement because these can be distracting. Make a time plan for your talk and have a watch or clock somewhere easy to see so that you tell how the time is going. Plan the ending to your talk in some detail, perhaps a quotation or another story summing up and making a final point. If your ending is well prepared you can skip to it if time seems to be running out. Allow time for questions at the end of the talk. It can sometimes be a good idea to get people to discuss what they heard in pairs or groups of three before asking questions.

Case studies

Discussion in small groups can centre on case studies contributed by different members of staff asked to pose a problem which they are encountering in the classroom. This needs careful preparation beforehand involving those concerned in setting out in writing the problem they are offering.

Collecting ideas

This activity involves taking a number of topics (as many as there are people in the group) and writing each at the head of an overhead projector transparency. For example, you could identify a number of aims for teaching in your subject. The transparencies are then passed round, with each person writing down an idea to meet the particular aim. At the end of the session the transparencies are projected and discussed and the best ideas incorporated into a record of the session. This can be done simply with sheets of paper, but using transparencies has the advantage that they can be shown to the whole group at once.

Information exchange

Course members are asked to bring with them information about how they do particular things – for example, how they keep records of children's progress. They then exchange information in groups of three. This is a particularly useful activity if people do not arrive together since groups can be formed as people arrive. The groups can then be asked to report to the whole group on the most useful ideas coming out of their discussion.

Evaluating and following up the event

It is a good idea to ask colleagues to complete an evaluation sheet on how they viewed the event. It may also be valuable to ask teachers to work in pairs to consider what they will do to implement what they have learned. The pairs can then meet later to discuss what they have done and help each other to evaluate the outcomes. There is also a case for following up the event in a meeting by asking people what they have tried as a result of it and the effect of this.

It is worth considering the possible benefits of continuing professional development and assessing whether the opportunities you are providing are achieving them. Glover and Law suggest that good professional development should lead to:

- more coherent planning and decision-making, with greater ownership of developments;
- improved staff skills;
- improved monitoring;
- improved motivation and team work;
- an improved teaching and learning focus;
- a 'questioning' culture;
- improved needs identification. (1996)

Pressures and costs of professional development

In planning for professional development you need to take the following into account:

- the pressure on time, both the time needed for professional development activities and the time needed to spread ideas;
- the funding available; there is usually a problem of how to finance the professional development opportunities needed;
- the disruption to teaching if teachers take time out for in-service opportunities;
- cynicism about professional development on the part of some colleagues.

QUESTIONS FOR CONSIDERATION

1 Does this school have a culture that teachers should be learners?

2 What opportunities are available for helping teachers to learn in my subject?

3 What opportunities am I providing to help teachers to learn in my subject?

4 What am I doing to help teachers achieve the aims we have agreed for the subject?

5 What learning needs do my colleagues feel they have?

6 What additional learning needs have I identified in my colleagues which they have not identified themselves?

7 What opportunities am I providing to encourage colleagues to reflect on their work?

8 What feedback have we from children about the way they feel about what they are learning?

9 Are there opportunities for people to observe each other teaching?

10 Do we do enough sharing of ideas? Could we do more?

11 How successful have the in-service events I have arranged been in improving the practice of teachers in the classroom?

CHAPTER 8

Supporting colleagues

A major task for you as subject leader is to support your colleagues in the teaching of your subject. To do this effectively you need to know them well as people, becoming aware of their ideas about teaching and their educational values, the level of self-esteem each one enjoys, and their confidence about teaching your subject. You also need to show that you care about them as people. This knowledge will enable you to be sensitive to their needs and perceptive in knowing the kind of help and advice they may need.

Climate of trust

It is easier to be helpful to others if the climate of the school is one of trust where people feel they can be open with each other and turn readily to each other for help. Blandford suggests that:

> In an open supportive communication climate, staff feel valued, crises are dealt with and staff are more open themselves. They will trusted, secure and confident in their jobs and in the organisation as a whole. Effective team-working, flexibility and a sense on involvement all contribute to, and benefit from, an open and supportive climate. (1997:56)

Even if this is not the climate in your school, you can do a certain amount to create a mini-climate for your subject. People are more likely to turn to you for help if you sometimes turn to them and acknowledge that you too have problems from time to time. This will not be seen as a weakness unless you do it too often but a readiness to learn from others which may encourage them to be ready to learn from you.

Types of support

Support can be of various kinds. It can be simply a readiness to help if you are asked about a problem. You may then be able to offer advice and suggestions, perhaps providing resources or offering your colleagues the opportunity to see what you are doing about a similar problem. You need to be seen as caring for your colleagues. You may, for example, become aware of a need to help because someone seems depressed about work. There may be a situation where a colleague appears to be failing and needs support in overcoming his or her difficulties. Newly qualified teachers need a lot of support during their induction year and the person who is acting as induction tutor may ask you to help. It is all a matter of being sensitive to other people and their problems and making them aware that you are ready to help if they wish it. It is important not to be dogmatic or unwilling to listen to the other person's point of view.

Part of your task as subject leader is to introduce colleagues to different aspects of your subject. You may do this incidentally and informally or as part of an in-service programme. This will also involve you in helping others to identify their professional development needs. Support may also be a matter of collaborative planning, perhaps with a pair or group of teachers with classes of the same age group or acting as a critical friend helping others to identify progress.

It is important that your attempts to help don't appear to be overtly judgemental or evaluative. If people think you are sitting in judgement on them when you try to help they will not turn to you. The emphasis needs to be on problem-solving and any necessary criticism should be open and honest and clearly an attempt to help.

There may also be a case for deliberate coaching in which you explain and demonstrate a particular approach to a colleague, perhaps a newly qualified teacher, taking a lesson in which you aim to demonstrate specific skills and techniques while the teacher watches. You then help this teacher as he or she tries out a similar approach in his or her own classroom. Your colleague may need direction and structure at the beginning of trying something new and feedback on how he or she is doing. You may also team-teach with someone else as a way of introducing new ways of working. Both these approaches require extra time for you to work together. You may also find that you need to spend time helping a colleague to learn how to use new resources.

Telford quotes a subject leader on the value of sharing success:

> I try to be really supportive of staff. I encourage people – can I help? Is there anything I can do? Valuing other people's point of view is important too – to get people to feel wanted and part of things – actively bringing people into the conversation. (1996:62)

There may be occasions when you need to act in a counselling role. A colleague may have a problem which is not easy to solve and your task will be to listen carefully, talk through the situation and lead that person to his or her own conclusions. You need to be accepting of the other person and avoid moralising or prescribing or appearing to be in any way threatening. Help your colleague to express his or her feelings about the situation. Don't try to impose your values but be sensitive to the other person's self-esteem. Ask open-ended questions but don't talk too much yourself. Offer reassurance and understanding. Don't offer ready-made solutions and offer any suggestions tentatively and gradually draw out your colleague's ideas about possible solutions and help in weighing them up and so lead towards a conclusion. Agree an action plan and make it clear that you are always ready to talk further.

You may find from time to time that you have to deal with people who are difficult. They may be hostile to your approaches and appear uninterested in your subject. You need to be assertive with such people and look for ways of being friendly. Some people tend to be negative about other people's ideas. They may respond negatively to any suggestion. Try not to get depressed about this. Analyse the problems under discussion with the person concerned and explore possible courses of action to see if you can find an acceptable way forward. There is also the kind of person who sounds enthusiastic about everything but in practice does nothing. Work with them to find a way that they can go forward successfully. Set deadlines and try to keep them.

Newton and Tarrant suggest that there is value in teachers reflecting on times when they felt supported in their work. The discussion about this might include:

- good listening for enough time, in a situation that has privacy, confidentiality and comfort as its key components. Listening skills will need to include positive non-verbal communication in areas such as posture, vocal tone and eye contact;
- practical helping;
- promoting, sponsoring, acknowledging and praising;
- counselling where appropriate;
- non-verbal support: smiling, nodding, thumbs up and so on;
- granting time to work on something. (1992:209)

Relationships

The relationships you normally have with colleagues will determine how ready they are to consult you. As subject leader you need to be on the look-out for good work in your subject and offer appropriate recognition and praise. Telling people they are doing well when this is the case does much to foster good relationships. It is important to recognise serious attempts at innovation even when they are not altogether successful because this is the way that people will be encouraged to try to improve their performance.

Your relationship with your head teacher and senior management team are also important. You need to keep them informed of how work in your subject is going and the plans you have for further development. It is also worth remembering that head teachers are as vulnerable as anyone else and rarely get told that they are doing well. Well-chosen words of thanks for support and help from the head teacher are likely to be well received.

You also need to have good relationships with other subject leaders, since you will be taking it in turns to be leaders and followers. As a newly appointed subject leader you can learn a lot from the way that experienced subject leaders work. You will know from the reactions of other colleagues which subject leaders are successful in developing the work in their subject and you can observe how they do this and see what ideas you can adopt in your own work.

Communication

Much depends on your ability as a communicator. You may need to communicate to inform, to explain, persuade, encourage, thank, consult and for many other purposes. Communication can go wrong in all sorts of ways. Words can mean different things to different people, depending on their experience. People can have emotional reactions which get in the way of their understanding a communication fully. They sometimes hear only what they want to hear and miss out on parts of the message. Communication needs to be seen as a two-way process, with those receiving the communication giving feedback about their views and ideas and feelings. There is often a need to negotiate a message so that it can be fully understood and acted upon. The characteristics of the person receiving a message determine how accurately it is received.

When you are communicating verbally your tone of voice and body language will affect the way the message comes across. You will also get feedback from the body language of those receiving the message. Facial expression, body movement as well as tone of voice and words chosen are all part of the communication process and you need to be sensitive not only to the message you are communicating but also to the way it is being received. People filter the messages they receive through their own feelings about both the message and the person who is sending it.

When you are trying to help another person you need to be an active listener. Sit so that you can see each other's face easily and read the body language. You show you are listening by your body posture, by keeping eye contact and by facial expression. You encourage your colleague to continue by nods and smiles, sounds of agreement and probing questions. You need to give him or her time to reflect by allowing some silences for thinking. You then need from time to time to reflect back what the other person has been saying to see if you have understood correctly, paraphrasing what you have heard. Avoid interrupting or asking leading questions. Instead ask questions such as 'Can you tell me more about that?' or 'How do you feel about that?'. Don't rush in with advice or detailed description of how you dealt with a similar situation. There may be a place for this, but after the other person has explored his or her own ideas about possible ways ahead.

Be alert to the body language of your colleague. He or she may signal emotional involvement, tension, discomfort, embarrassment or anxiety by his or her sitting position, facial expression, frowning, by dropping eye contact or by dryness of mouth. Lack of interest may be signalled by losing eye contact, fidgeting or looking at a watch or clock.

Supporting new teachers

From time to time you will need to be concerned with inducting a new teacher into the ways of the school and how your subject is taught in the school. Any teacher coming new to the school needs induction into the work of the school and the work of each subject area. You need to talk with a new colleague to find out how happy he or she is with teaching your subject and find out how far his or her previous work is similar to the work you are advocating in your subject and what support is likely to be needed. You need to make it clear that you are ready to help with any problems and are ready to offer support when it is needed. You will also need to provide the new teacher with any documents you have produced about your subject and introduce him or her to the resources available for the subject and explain how to access them. You need to find out tactfully how confident the teacher feels about the subject and make it clear that you are always ready to help if necessary. You may need to help to define a new colleague's professional development needs in your subject and look for ways in which you can

> **CASE STUDY**
>
> Marie was a teacher from New Zealand who had recently come to England to fill a teaching post in an area where there was a serious shortage of teachers. She had had to learn about the National Curriculum and the literacy and numeracy strategies, and David, who was the mathematics subject leader, set out to help her. The local authority also laid on a course for teachers newly arrived from overseas and she was on a steep learning curve.
>
> David first of all spent time talking with her about the mathematics curriculum as it applied to the age group she was teaching and the structure of the numeracy hour. He also plied her with questions about the ways things were done in New Zealand and how she had taught mathematics in her school there. This was very interesting and gave him some new ideas about his own work. He then arranged for her to observe one of his mathematics lessons, having previously talked her through the work he intended to do. She was impressed with the skill the children were showing in manipulating numbers and liked the three-part plan of the lesson.
>
> David then arranged with the head teacher some time when he could observe her teaching and make suggestions. He had worked through the lesson plan with her in advance and knew exactly what she was planning to do. The lesson went well and he felt that she had made a good start and the children were learning.

provide opportunities for new learning.

Supporting the newly qualified teacher

A newly qualified teacher may need more help and you will want to liaise with the induction tutor to ensure that any help you offer fits into a planned programme. The teacher may need support in preparing and structuring lessons, teaching at an appropriate level and catering for all abilities, classroom organisation, and management and discipline problems. You may find that you can best support through some joint planning, giving the teacher the opportunity to observe your lessons or suggesting observing other teachers who teach the subject particularly well. There is also a case for arranging informal discussions to review progress and sort out problems.

Newly qualified teachers are likely to need support from all the subject leaders so you will have to be careful not to overload them with advice, while making it clear that you are there to help when needed. You also need to liaise with whoever is responsible for mentoring them. Kemp and Nathan suggest that they may need support in:

- preparing and structuring of lessons;

- classroom organisation and management;
- relationships with pupils, and discipline problems with either individuals or groups;
- coping with the pressure of work;
- following school assessment policies. (1989:190, 191)

Part of the induction of newly qualified teachers involves observing other people teach, and they will have time set aside for this. When planning a lesson to be observed you need to consider how the focus you could offer for the observation relates to the requirements for the satisfactory completion of the induction period. It is helpful if you can plan a lesson which incorporates aspects of teaching which the teacher is particularly concerned about and talk about this in advance so that he or she is aware of points to look out for.

Stress

Teaching is a stressful occupation and you need both to be aware of stress in yourself and stress in your colleagues. Teachers are likely to be stressed by pressure of work and the time available in which to do it, pupil attitudes and behaviour, lack of administrative support, lack of resources, large classes and so on. Most teachers find an OFSTED inspection stressful. A person may also be stressed because of events in his or her personal life, such as illness in the family, marriage breakdown, problems with children and other concerns. Stress can lead to a lack of motivation for work, negativism, irritability and tendency to blame others for things which are unsatisfactory. You need to be sensitive to indicators of stress. Fleming and Amesbury note that someone suffering from stress is likely to exhibit some or all of the following symptoms:

- a general deterioration in performance at work;
- an increase in sickness absence, which may fall into a particular pattern of frequent short periods of absence, possibly due to stress symptoms such as headaches, difficulty in breathing, poor sleep patterns, indigestion and palpitations;
- an increase in irritability resulting in conflict and tension with other colleagues and a deterioration in relationships;
- loss of motivation and job satisfaction;
- less contact with people outside work;
- in some cases, over-eating and/or an increase in alcohol consumption. (2001:150)

Stress is likely to be less when people feel supported and appreciated in their work and everyone in a leadership role can help by providing support and appreciation. It is important that people suffering from stress are not made to feel guilty. Stress is particularly likely to occur at times of change, and team involvement in managing change will help to avoid this.

QUESTIONS FOR CONSIDERATION

1 Do people in this school consult easily with others about the problems they are encountering?

2 Are other teachers ready to talk to me about their problems?

3 Am I sufficiently sensitive towards other people's problems?

4 What am I doing to help other teachers teach my subject?

5 Do I do enough to encourage people? When did I last praise someone's work? When did I last thank someone?

6 Am I a good listener?

7 Do I do enough to support teachers new to the school and newly qualified teachers?

CHAPTER 9

Managing resources

Part of your job as a subject leader will be managing the resources needed for your subject. This involves the following:

- maintaining an inventory of all the materials and equipment available in the school for the teaching of your subject;
- keeping an overview of the ICT resources available for your subject and helping teachers to use them;
- organising storage and a system for accessing materials and equipment;
- maintaining materials and equipment in good order and noting what needs replacing each year;
- making decisions in collaboration with colleagues about how any money available for resources for the subject should be spent.

There is quite a lot of work involved in fulfilling these obligations, which will vary according to the demands of your subject. If it is possible, help from a teaching assistant should be sought. Many of the tasks involved can easily be done by non-teaching staff, and some, such as maintaining and repairing books and materials, might be done by parent volunteers. Look for what help you can find.

Maintaining an inventory

It is important that you know exactly what resources are available and that this information is widely shared with other teachers. If no such inventory exists you need to start by listing everything, noting where it is stored, its state of repair and whether it needs replacing. This may not be as easy as it sounds! Much material will be in teachers' classrooms and they may feel possessive about their resources and suspicious about everyone knowing what they have. You need to ask them to list, or allow you or a teaching assistant to list what they have, identifying any material which they use very little, so that this can be made available to someone else if it is needed, and also noting anything which should be replaced. You also need to list any materials stored centrally. When the list is complete, copies of it, with information about where each item is housed, can be made available to all teachers so that they know where to turn when they want something.

When your list is complete, consider how it relates to what you think desirable by way of resources for your subject and start to think about your priorities when money becomes available. You can then take advantage of any opportunity which arises for increasing the resource stock.

Organising storage and a system for accessing resources

Resources need to be stored in ways that make them easily accessible. Some of them will be stored in classrooms in ways that suit the classroom teacher, but centrally stored resources are your responsibility and they need to be clearly labelled and stored in such a way that they are easy to find and easy to keep in order. Some schools use topic boxes for some aspects of work, with all that is needed for work on a particular topic in science, for example, or technology, collected together in a large container with a list of what is there so that teachers can check the materials back when they have finished with them. Video and audio tapes, slides and computer software need careful cataloguing and labelling so that people can easily find what they need. The numbers of any sets of books should be clearly labelled so that teachers can check when they borrow them that every one has been collected.

It may also be worth getting teachers to compare notes about the way they store and display resources in their classrooms and how they make them available to children. Technology teachers may have a pegboard for tools with an outline of where each tool should go marked so that the teacher can easily see if anything is missing. Boxes containing materials and equipment can have a list of what should be inside on the lid so that the contents can be checked. Cupboard shelves can have marked spaces for particular items so that children can see where to put things when they have used them. The resources stored in each classroom can have a coloured label on them, different for each class to show which classroom they came from if they are borrowed. Good ideas for storage and systems for use can be passed on. It is particularly helpful to exchange ideas about how to keep resources in good order in the classroom. One way of doing this is to make each shelf or worktop display the responsibility of one or more children whose task it is to check what should be there at the end of each session.

In organising the storage it is a good idea to think how often any particular resource will be used. Those used most frequently need to be stored with easy access in mind. Fleming and Amesbury suggest that when teaching resources are regularly used by several team members the following questions might be asked about possible locations:

- Can people get it without disturbing someone's lesson?
- Can it be reached without shifting other things?
- If sheets are used, are they kept in files, boxes or a filing cabinet?
- If books, can they easily be transported from room to room? Remember health and safety may be an issue here.
- If AV equipment, is the location secure and safe?
- Does the choice of location inconvenience some colleagues more than others?
- Who will keep track of resources? How? (2001:108)

You also need to think about the need for teachers to book resources in frequent use and to provide a system for doing this. There should be a signing out system for all centrally held resources so that at any time you can track down something which is wanted urgently.

The whole task of storing and caring for resources is one which teaching assistants can well undertake.

Maintaining materials and equipment

Resources need maintenance. Books may have loose pages which need to be repaired. Tools may need sharpening. Worksheets may need to be replaced. Physical education apparatus may become unsafe. What is needed by way of maintenance varies from subject to subject and is more important in some subjects than others, particularly where health and safety issues are concerned. Much of the maintenance work could be done by a group of parent volunteers, perhaps working with a teaching assistant.

There is also a need to stock-take resources at least annually. This means having a complete inventory and checking whether everything listed is still there, still in use and in good condition. This should be a preliminary to planning what new resources are needed. Once again, this could be done by a teaching assistant under your guidance.

Making decisions about new resources

Schools will have different arrangements for making decisions about what should be added to the resource collection. In large schools, each subject may have its own budget, and your task, in collaboration with colleagues, will be to decide how to spend it. In smaller schools teachers may have to bid for a share in the school's budget. In both cases you will need to consider what is needed and what should be the priorities for spending. Your priorities should be determined by the priorities in your development plan.

You also need to think about the demands of your subject on consumable materials. This will be particularly relevant for technology and art, and to some extent for science, and you will need to consider how much material you need for the coming year and plan how teachers can get access to it. You will need to keep an eye on how quickly it gets used to ensure that you do not end the year without enough material.

You will be able to find out what is available from catalogues, and in some areas from occasional exhibitions by educational contractors. Teachers may also see particular resources during an in-service course or at a teachers' centre or in a library. The task will be to weigh up the value of particular materials considering their cost, appropriateness, durability and shelf life, interest and stimulation. You will need to think about how they fit in with other materials already in use.

Planning for new resources is a task which you need to undertake with colleagues, meeting to consider proposals and prioritise them, considering the effect of each carefully and looking at any training needs the teachers will have in preparing for their use. It is helpful at this stage to consider what will be the result of the new resources in terms of improvement in children's learning. This will give you criteria by which to judge whether you have bought wisely. Discussion of resources provides a good opportunity for discussing teaching approaches.

When you have decided on what to buy and have received it and put it into use you need to monitor what happens to see whether it is being used in a satisfactory way and whether it is leading to improved learning by children.

While administrative staff will send out the orders and keep records of what is ordered, you need to keep some records of your own. Fleming and Amesbury suggest that you keep a simple grid sheet with the following headings for columns:

- date (the date which the order was placed);
- received (tick this column when items ordered have been received);
- details (include the supplier's name, catalogue reference number and brief description of the order);
- estimated cost;
- actual cost (as invoiced – this may include price changes, postage and packing etc.);
- balance (use pencil to write the balance based on estimated cost and then use pen when the actual cost is known). (2001:111)

Subject issues

Subjects will vary in the demands they make for resources and in the effect of their use. In teaching technology, teachers need to be aware of safety issues and take time to teach children to use tools safely. If you are technology subject leader you need to ensure that all teachers are competent in the use of the tools needed and know how to work safely with them. You need good storage for tools and materials, and children need to be trained in their use. If cooking is involved, are the children being trained to be careful of heat sources? This may also be necessary in science if the work you are doing involves heat.

Physical education subject leaders also need to be conscious of the need to ensure that children in all classes are using apparatus safely and are moving it in safe ways.

QUESTIONS FOR CONSIDERATION

1   Have I an inventory of all the resources the school possesses for my subject, giving where they are stored? Do all teachers have access to a copy of it?

2   Are resources that are held centrally stored in a way that makes access easy? Do I need any more containers, cupboards or filing cabinets?

3   Do teachers exchange ideas about the best way of storing and using the resources kept in their classrooms?

4   Is there a system for borrowing from the central collection or from other classes?

5   What am I doing to maintain the collection in good repair? Can I enlist help in doing this from parents?

6   How comprehensive is the collection of resources we have? What are the priorities for new purchases or replacements?

7   Am I doing anything to evaluate the use made of the resources we have and any new ones we buy?

8   Do I review resources at regular intervals?

9   Can I enlist help from teaching assistants or parent volunteers?

CHAPTER 10

Monitoring the work of other teachers

Probably the most difficult task for subject leaders is that of monitoring the subject work of other teachers, and OFSTED reports suggest that this is the weakest element in the work of most subject leaders. It is difficult because time for it is hard to find and there can be an element of threat in it which you have to try hard to overcome. It is important to see it as something positive – a way of discovering how to offer help to others most successfully. It is nevertheless an important part of being a subject leader. As with so many aspects of the role it can be helped or hindered by the school climate. If this is one in which people look to each other for help and trust each other to help in positive ways it is much easier to find out how others are doing. Whatever the climate, you need to establish the idea that you are there to help and encourage. This will be easier if you are in the habit of recognising and celebrating your colleagues' achievements in the classroom.

West suggests that subject leaders need to monitor what is happening so that they may:

- acknowledge contributions of staff in implementing agreed policies;
- celebrate and share good practice;
- maintain commitment to building quality into the curriculum-in-action;
- engage in informed dialogue on specific aspects of practice;
- extend existing insight into the complexities of teaching and learning and go below the surface of classroom practice;
- generate a common language relating to teaching and learning;
- identify and provide what forms of support and development are needed;
- extend teacher repertoires. (1998:47)

In particular you need to know whether the work being carried out is meeting the National Curriculum requirements. You should therefore be monitoring the value and effectiveness of the following:

- the long-term and short-term goals the teacher is aiming for;
- the teacher's command of the subject;
- the planning, evaluating and recording of children's progress in the subject;

- the children's development of relevant skills, concepts, knowledge and understanding;
- the way work is being marked and the feedback being given to children;
- the way children's progress and achievement are being assessed and the way assessments are being used to inform teaching;
- the teaching approaches which are being adopted – the place of exposition, questioning, discussion, etc.
- the way the class is being organised – the use of whole-class teaching, group and individual work;
- the extent to which there is differentiation of work to match the needs of the most and least able and children of different backgrounds;
- the provision of homework and the way it is marked;
- the way time and other resources are being used.

Forms of monitoring

There are quite a number of ways in which you can find out how your subject is being taught. The following might be tried.

Exchange of classes

One useful approach which gets over the time problem to some extent, is to arrange with another subject leader to exchange classes for a lesson so that you each can make a judgement about how well the teaching of your subject is going. You will still need to spend time before the lesson finding out what your colleague has been doing, what he or she would most like you to look at and giving him or her similar information about your work. You can then spend time together afterwards exchanging information about your findings and helping each other plan ahead.

Team teaching

This has the disadvantage that time is needed for two teachers to work together but is a less threatening way of getting to know how a colleague teaches than direct classroom observation. It can be a most valuable way of helping a teacher who is hesitant about teaching your subject, but in this situation you may not find out how the teacher works when alone in the classroom. However, you will find out something of what the children are learning and have the chance to look at their work.

Studying teachers' plans

Teachers' plans for their work in your subject will also tell you a good deal and it may be possible to have a meeting at which everyone, including you, describes his or her plans and goals for the next half-term. This can offer an opportunity for people to make suggestions to each other and raise any problems they see in each other's plans.

Studying children's work

You can also learn a good deal about what is happening from looking at children's work. Classroom displays are often informative about what has been happening and it may be worth while asking teachers if you can look at a cross-section of children's work with a sample from the most and least able and those in the middle. Looking at a cross-section of work may also be a topic for a meeting with each teacher, showing the work of perhaps three children and everyone offering suggestions to others about how the work can be developed and improved.

Studying children's views

You can also learn from the children themselves. If you exchange a class with another subject leader you can spend some time asking the children about what they have been studying, what they enjoyed, what they found difficult, which activities they most liked and which they disliked, what they thought about the subject. You can also do this with older children by giving them a questionnaire which asks similar questions. Once again, it can be a good idea to discuss this with the staff group and get everyone to survey their class and then compare notes on the findings.

Talking with individuals

You will also learn from discussion with individual teachers. This may be an informal chat when you see someone, but you need to be sure that you find time to talk to everyone and it may be a good idea to schedule a series of meetings for such discussions. Teachers might be encouraged to bring their plans and records to these meetings, which should give you a good idea of what is happening.

Studying tapes of classroom work

Another possibility is to agree with colleagues to tape some aspect of their work in the classroom such as a questioning session and then to listen to this and discuss it with a group. It may be a good idea to do this yourself as a starting point.

Studying the outcomes of testing and teacher assessment

In the case of Years 2 and 6 you will have information from the Standard Assessment Tasks for assessing attainment in English and mathematics. Your school may also use optional tests at other stages which will give you information. Teachers will also have tested children's progress in some other subjects and may be able to give you information about this. They will also have records of individual children's progress which they may be prepared to share with you

Classroom observation

While classroom observation is a very important part of the monitoring process, it is perhaps the most difficult aspect to fulfil, partly because of the time needed. You will need to arrange with your head teacher an opportunity to see other members of staff in action. It also needs careful handling because it can be seen as threatening. You can make it seem less threatening by the way you approach it. Research suggests that where teachers see classroom observation as part of action research they tend to welcome it rather than find it a cause for concern. It may help to set observation in such a context by emphasising the fact that you are there to help rather than to judge.

You need to have a pre-observation discussion in which you consider the following:

- The objectives and plans the teacher has for the lesson and the way it will be taught.
- The focus of the observation. You need to give the teacher the opportunity to suggest the observations which would be most useful to him or her in developing his or her work and then make clear the other things you will be looking for.
- The way your presence in the class will be explained to the children.
- Where you will sit for the formal parts of the lesson.
- Whether you would like to have some time at the end of the lesson to talk to the children about what they have learned.
- The arrangements for a feedback session, which should be as soon after the observation as you can manage.

During the lesson you may decide to concentrate on the focus the teacher suggests and just note any other points that seem relevant, or you may prefer to observe more widely. It is a good idea to decide in advance what you will look for and limit your observations to some extent. The following is a comprehensive list of things you might look for from which you can select:

- the lesson objectives and their communication to the children;
- the overall organisation of the classroom as a learning environment;
- the way the teacher has planned for class, group and individual learning and the effectiveness of these approaches;
- the way the teacher has planned for the range of ability within the class and the effectiveness of this provision;

- the children's engagement with the work in hand;
- the teacher's subject knowledge;
- the teaching methods chosen and their suitability;
- the teacher's skill in exposition and in questioning;
- the resources available and their use;
- the way the teacher controls the children;
- the use of praise and encouragement for effort as well achievement;
- the use of time;
- the involvement of any support staff;
- points at which the teacher interacted positively, negatively or neutrally with children;
- the teacher behaviours which seemed to facilitate learning and which impeded it;
- the use of assessment;
- did the lesson meet the stated objectives?
- the way the lesson ended – did the teacher draw together what had been learned?
- what aspects of this lesson were successful and why, and what aspects were less successful and why;
- the teacher's relationships with the children;
- possible ways of following up this lesson.

You need to consider how you will record what you see. You can do this by having an agreed format which you can share with the teacher or you can make field notes of things as they occur to you. It is helpful to note the timing of a lesson as it goes on, noting the time at which activities change.

CASE STUDY

Ross was in his second year of teaching and was responsible for a Year 3 class. When Jenny, who was the subject leader for science, said she would like to observe one of his lessons, he suggested that it would be very helpful if she would look critically at his questioning technique since this was an area which interested him and which he was trying to develop in an attempt to help his children think more scientifically.

She agreed to make this the focus of her observation and started by making a plan of the classroom showing where each boy and girl was sitting. She then used this to plot where Ross's questions were directed. She recorded each question and noted whether it was a question to see whether the children could recall what they had learned or one which demanded original thinking at a higher level. She noted the length of time Ross gave for children to think about each question before asking someone to answer. She also noted the way in which Ross responded to answers given, recording whether his response was positive, negative or neutral, paying particular attention to responses where the answer was wrong.

This gave her a good picture of how Ross was using questioning. She found that he was quite good at giving children time to think about their answers, but her plan of who answered, which she shared with him, showed that he tended to call on children seated within a triangle with him at the apex, rarely calling on children seated at the extreme right and left front sides of the classroom. He asked boys and girls for answers in fairly equal numbers.

His questions were about equally divided between those testing previous knowledge and those which called for new thinking, and the children responded well to the latter and came up with a number of original ideas. He tended to be quite good at making positive responses to interesting answers but his weakest area was in the way he dealt with wrong answers. He simply said that they were wrong without exploring the child's thinking or making the statement seem less of a put-down. Jenny noticed that children who had been told their answers were wrong did not put up their hands so frequently afterwards.

Ross found the feedback very valuable and planned to put what he had learned into action as soon as possible.

After the lesson you need to have a discussion with the teacher about what you have observed. Try to make this as relaxed as possible by meeting somewhere reasonably comfortable where you cannot be disturbed. It may be a good idea to ask the teacher to start the discussion by giving his or her account of what seemed to be happening, with an assessment of how well the outcomes met the objectives of the lesson. You can then give your account of what you felt was happening, making this as positive as possible, first of all highlighting the strengths and the areas which were successful and then talking about those which need developing further. Give examples from your notes to illustrate the points you are making. It is useful to consider why things happened: what caused some misbehaviour at one point, for example, or why children were reluctant to answer particular questions. This may lead to a discussion of the way the teacher's behaviour encouraged or impeded learning and what might be done to produce even better results. End the discussion by considering what should happen in the next lesson in this subject and how the work you have observed could be followed up.

One problem which sometimes arises in post-observation conferences, particularly where things have not gone well, is that the teacher concerned becomes very defensive, perhaps blaming the pupils. The best way to deal with this is to acknowledge that the teacher has to deal with problems, stress the need to look for ways of overcoming them and look for things which the teacher can actually do to make things better. You may also have to deal with failure which the teacher may acknowledge. The head teacher will be aware of this and there may already be a programme of help in operation and you will need to take account of this in any work you plan to help the teacher concerned in teaching your subject. If it fits with the school's plan for the teacher, some team teaching may help or the teacher may benefit from observing you at work. Look for any positive signs which can be built upon.

In your observation you need to be aware that there are a number of possible sources of error. You need to be aware of this and check out your observations with the teacher in the post-observation discussion. Errors in observation may include the following:

- What happens at the beginning of the lesson has undue influence on what you see later.
- You make unfounded assumptions about what you are seeing – you need to check these out in the post-observation discussion.
- You do not sufficiently take into account the effect of your presence in the classroom on the teacher, who may be nervous about being observed.
- Having another person in the classroom also changes the climate so that children may show off for your benefit.
- You make judgements on too small a sample.
- You do not take your personal beliefs and values into account sufficiently and they may bias your judgement about someone who works in a different way from you. You tend to see what you want to see.

Outcomes of monitoring

As subject leader you should be able to obtain a picture of the way your subject is being taught and learned throughout the school. You may need to report on this to your head teacher who should certainly be kept informed. This will probably be in the context of the school's programme of performance management. You may also need to report to OFSTED inspectors or local authority advisers from time to time. It is a good idea to make yourself an annual programme of monitoring, doing a certain amount each term depending on the time that can be made available for you to observe other people. You should get from your monitoring a clear picture of the development needs of your colleagues which should help you to provide training for them yourself and help you to assess the value of courses on offer in the area which they might attend.

QUESTIONS FOR CONSIDERATION

1 What am I doing to monitor the work of colleagues in my subject?

2 How well do I know what is going on in my subject across the school?

3 Do we celebrate and share good practice?

4 Is work in my subject improving generally? How do I know this?

5 What support am I providing for colleagues as a result of monitoring?

6 What are colleagues gaining from my classroom observation?

7 Am I managing to avoid error in classroom observation?

8 What training needs does my monitoring suggest?

9 Have I kept the head teacher informed about my overall findings?

CHAPTER 11

Managing change

As a subject leader you will be concerned to some extent with managing change. Even if the work in the subject you lead is overall pretty good, you will still need to be thinking ahead to ways in which the work can be developed further.

When you are first a subject leader you may have many questions about the work in your subject, the answers to which will lead to change. Bell and Ritchie suggest that you might ask yourself the following:

> Is the policy and scheme of work appropriate and up-to-date? Is everyone using the scheme effectively? What changes could be introduced to improve children's learning throughout the school? Which colleagues need help and how can they be supported effectively? In what ways can difficult situations be resolved? Do the resources need updating and making more accessible? In what other ways might the subject be developed in the school over the next few years? (1999:1)

The answers to these questions and others will inevitably lead to change, and colleagues will need to be supported as new ways of doing things are introduced. Change will still be something to consider as you become involved in your role as subject leader and you will be thinking about how the work can be developed further. Change in this context is synonymous with development.

Fullan defines change as it affects the individual as follows:

> Change at the individual level is a process whereby individuals alter their ways of *thinking* and *doing* (e.g. teaching in this case). It is a process of developing new *skills* and, above all, of finding *meaning* and *satisfaction* in new ways of doing things. (1985:396)

You need to take a positive attitude to change and encourage your colleagues to see it in a positive light also. Innovation can be interesting and exciting and can lead to teachers having greater confidence in themselves. It can lead to personal development and to improved learning on the part of children. The idea is to create a climate in which colleagues are happy to try out new ways of doing things and learn from each other by discussing the results. You need to consider at an early stage your priorities for change and the best place to make a start. One way of starting to make changes is to try out something yourself and invite colleagues to assess the results. Or you might invite a colleague who is sympathetic to the sort of change you want to make to try something out and report back to the staff group. Another approach is to encourage action research in which teachers set out to study a particular way of working in their classes, observe the results and share their findings with colleagues. Action research is discussed in more detail in Chapter 16.

Rodd suggests that:

> Leadership for change requires vision and inspiration, careful planning. decision-making skill, effective communication, confident conflict management and sensitive handling of people involved or affected by the change. (1994:114)

Loucks-Horsley and Stiegelbauer make the following points about change:

- Change is a process, not an event. It takes time and is accomplished only in stages.
- Because the individual is a key player in the change process, his or her needs must be the focus of help and support designed to facilitate change. Organisations cannot change until the individuals within them change.
- Change is a highly personal experience. The people experiencing the change must be taken into account. Since change is made by individuals, their personal satisfactions, frustrations, concerns, motivations and perceptions all contribute to the success or failure of a change initiative.
- The change process is developmental. Individuals involved in change go through stages in their perceptions and feelings about an innovation, as well as in their skill and sophistication in using an innovation.
- Well-developed staff development results from a measure of *diagnostic/prescriptive* thinking. The most relevant and supportive staff development can be planned only if staff developers diagnose where participants are in the change process and design activities that resolve their expressed needs.
- Staff developers need to have a *systematic* view of change and constantly *adapt* their behaviours as the change progresses. They need to stay in constant touch with the progress of individuals in the context of the total organisation supporting the change.
- Everyone approaching a change, initially implementing an innovation, or developing skill in using an innovation, will have certain perceptions, feelings, motivations, frustrations and satisfactions about the innovation and change process. (1991:17–19)

Research suggests that people go through a series of stages in coming to terms with change. They start by trying to form a picture of what might be involved and try to fit this into their own frames of reference. They may be shocked by what is being suggested and try to minimise the effect it seems likely to have on their work. They may feel unhappy about the change and try to make sense of it and reconcile it to their own values and beliefs. Eventually they accept it as reality and start to examine ways in which they can work with it. They begin to see how they can work with the change and become confident in adapting and using new ways of working.

As subject leader you need to be aware of these stages and be ready to support your colleagues as they go through them, providing pressure to change as well as support in changing. You need to be ready for some people to resist change. You can minimise this by good communication, helping colleagues to understand the reasons why you are suggesting change. The more they are involved in planning for change the more likely it is that they will accept it and go along with new ways of working. You will need good listening skills, problem-solving skills and the ability to negotiate an agreement. You may be able to bargain by providing new materials which teachers are keen to have to support the change. You may find it helpful to make a force-field analysis – a technique devised by Lewin (1951) which involves considering the forces which are acting for and against you in planning something. Positive forces might be that teachers are not entirely happy with the way the subject has been led in the immediate past and are ready for a change. The head teacher is keen that you should develop the work in new ways and is prepared to support you by providing resources where they are needed and will encourage teachers to undertake further training where this is needed. Restraining forces may be the attitudes of some long-serving staff who are quite happy with the way they are working and don't want to make changes, the time that will be involved in selling ideas to others and discussing them, and the effort required to change long-term practices. You can then think about ways of overcoming the restraining forces and making the best use of the positive ones.

Fullan and Stiegelbauer give the following list of 'dos and don'ts' for change:

1. Do not assume that your version of what the change should be is the one that should or could be implemented. There should be interaction with those involved so that ideas are modified.
2. Assume that any significant innovation requires individual implementers to work out their own meaning. Effective implementation is a process of clarification.
3. Assume that conflict and disagreement are not only inevitable but fundamental to successful change.

4. Assume that people need pressure to change but it will be effective only under conditions that involve their reaction.

5. Assume that effective change takes time. Significant change can be expected to take two to three years.

6. Do not assume that the reason for lack of implementation is outright rejection of the values embedded in the change or hard-core resistance. Reasons can be varied.

7. Do not expect all or even most people and groups to change.

8. Assume that you will need a plan that is based on the above assumptions and that addresses the factors known to affect implementation.

9. Assume that no amount of homework will ever make it totally clear what action should be taken.

10. Assume that changing the culture of institutions is the real agenda, not implementing single innovations. (1991:105–8)

It is also worth remembering that real change is a slow process. There is often a low point after about half a term, when things don't seem to be working very well and people are feeling that things were better before they started the change. You need to be very supportive at this stage and encourage people to persist and win through to the next stage where things start to work.

CASE STUDY

Newtown Friars Primary School served a large village and had only 104 children divided into four classes. This meant that each teacher, including the head, was a subject leader for at least two subjects. Barbara was subject leader for history and geography and worked hard to help her colleagues develop work in these two subjects. She decided that there were many ways in which the two subjects were related – they were both concerned with people and places and she felt that there was much to be said for taking a place or a theme and studying it from both points of view.

She talked to her colleagues about this and they were not very enthusiastic. They had the schemes of work for both subjects clearly worked out and had materials for them which might not fit if the emphasis were different. However, after a lot of discussion she persuaded the teacher of the class for children in Years 3 and 4 to try a local study which looked at both the history and geography of their village while she embarked with her Years 5 and 6 children on a study of the nearby town. There were a number of old buildings in the village, the church dated back to the fourteenth century, and there were also a number of old people in the village, some of them grandparents of the present children, who could tell them about life in the past. The children studied maps of the village and looked at the physical features of the neighbourhood and considered why the village had grown up there. The nearby town had a good museum as well as old buildings and exemplified a number of geographical concepts in that it had grown up there because of the river which brought certain industries to the town, and it was also a market town in the midst of farming country. The children studied past and present maps of the town and learned about the industry there and went on to compare it with a town of similar size in France.

Both these projects worked well. The children enjoyed them, and the exhibitions of work which resulted were of interest to parents. The success of the projects interested the other teachers who decided that they would look at ways of combining the two subjects with their classes.

Readiness to change and the effectiveness of the change process is affected by the context in which it occurs and the way in which the change is introduced. Teachers will be more ready to consider change when they can see a clear need for it and when what is being suggested is in accord with their values and beliefs about education. They need full information about what is being proposed. They will also be influenced by the success or otherwise of previous changes – there may be those who will say, 'We tried that some time ago and it didn't work.' They will be concerned about how much time and effort it involves and whether it involves acquiring new skills or fresh learning. There may be some who see it as a threat to the work they are already doing and there may be a fear of the unknown and of being de-skilled. They will also be affected by the degree of confidence they have in you as a teacher and the way you put your ideas across. It will help if the head teacher is behind your plans and is encouraging.

Key factors in successful change are the involvement of those concerned in every stage of planning, sensitive handling of people which takes account of their values, their ideas and anxieties, the right mixture of pressure, support and assistance, the provision of any necessary in-service support, recognition of progress in implementing the change, and the provision of appropriate resources.

QUESTIONS FOR CONSIDERATION

1 In what areas of work in my subject do I want to make changes?

2 What are the positive forces for change in the school?

3 How can I overcome the restraining forces?

4 What is my first priority for change? Where shall I start?

5 What is the best way of introducing the changes I want to make?

6 Which of my colleagues is likely to be sympathetic to the changes I want to suggest and which will be against it?

7 What is the best way to deal with those who are antagonistic to change?

8 What in-service training will be needed to support the changes? How can this be provided?

9 What resources will be needed to support the changes?

10 How shall we evaluate the effects of the changes? When shall we do this? What evidence shall we use?

CHAPTER 12

Evaluating and record-keeping

As subject leader you have a responsibility for making judgements about children's progress in your subject. The National Standards for Subject Leaders state that subject leaders should:

- establish and implement clear policies and practices for assessing, recording and reporting on pupil achievement, and for using this information to recognise achievement and to assist pupils in setting targets for further improvement;
- ensure that information about pupils' achievements in previous classes and schools is used effectively to secure good progress in the subject. (Teacher Training Agency 1998:11)

In Chapter 10 we looked at ways in which you might monitor the work of teachers. An important part of this is analysing data on pupils' attainment and reviewing with teachers their assessments of the progress children are making in their classes so that you are able to make judgements about how well the work is going. This means agreeing with teachers the kinds of records which will be kept. The actual format of the records may be different for different teachers, but they should all contain similar information.

Assessment of children's progress

Your school may have an assessment policy which sets out the kinds of assessments which teachers are expected to make, both of the work of individual children and also of the success or otherwise of their teaching. If the school does not have such a policy then you need to consider with your colleagues how work in your subject will be assessed. Schools are required to keep individual records of children, giving information about academic achievement, other skills and abilities, and progress made. These must be updated at least once a year.

The broader purposes of assessment, whether undertaken to meet the National Curriculum requirements or those of the teachers concerned, should include the following:

- to guide teachers in future planning;
- to monitor how well objectives are being achieved;
- to monitor the progress of each child and inform future teaching;

- to help children achieve and maintain high standards of work;
- to inform children about the progress of their learning and encourage them to learn further;
- to provide information for parents about their child's progress.

Assessment can be formative or summative. Formative assessment is the day-to-day evaluation of a child's work to diagnose learning needs and plan future teaching. Summative assessment is assessment at the end of stage of work or at regular periods during the year to assess what children know, understand and can do. The National Curriculum assessments are summative.

End of Key Stage assessments

Each teacher is required to make assessments of progress in the attainment targets of the National Curriculum for each child at the end of each Key Stage, and it is your responsibility to see that this happens and that assessments are done fairly and adequately. Some of your colleagues may need help with this, particularly any who are newly qualified, and where there is more than one class in a year group it will be important to see that teachers use similar criteria in assessing their children. The National Curriculum sets out requirements for each level of attainment in each subject and it is a good idea for teachers to help each other to make assessments of the level each child has reached. Teachers can act as moderators for each other and you can also act as a moderator. You need to ensure that each assessment is valid, i.e. it really assesses what it is intended to assess; and reliable, i.e. that you would come to a similar conclusion if the assessment were repeated.

The way teachers assess the learning and development of children will vary from subject to subject. The PE teacher will be making assessments from watching the performance of children; the English teacher will be assessing written work as well as assessing spoken contributions in class; teachers of technology and art will be assessing children's output and their skill in using tools and different media, and all teachers will be using a range of different observations to assess children's development and progress. You need to spend time with your colleagues, considering how best to evaluate what is happening in their classes and the work of individual children.

Another aspect of the evaluation of what is happening is the consideration of whether any groups of children are doing better or worse than other groups. Are boys doing worse or better than girls in your subject, and should anything be done if this is the case? How well are children with special educational needs and very able children doing? How well are children from ethnic minorities doing compared with the indigenous population? Have you any black Caribbean boys in your school? Research suggests that while they start school achieving well, their performance drops off as the years go by and they do less well than other children. Indian and Chinese children tend to do better than the average. Is this the case in your school? If so, should anything be done about it? It is easier to make these kinds of assessments of children's progress if teachers use a computer for recording in a number of areas of their work. You need to think about how computer records would help in recording progress in your subject.

Marking

One of the issues you will need to consider for some subjects is marking. Ideally there should be a policy for the whole school on this so that children know what to expect, particularly as they grow older. There are two important aspects of this. The way teachers mark work should provide feedback to children, and the teacher also needs a record of what each child has achieved.

Where written work is concerned, children should know what the teacher thinks about it and where there are mistakes to be corrected; and with older children there can be a system of symbols to mark errors such as those of spelling or punctuation. The most valuable aspect of marking is the written message giving encouragement and praise for specific aspects of the work where appropriate and suggesting ways in which it could be improved if this is relevant. Teachers then need to think about what they are going to record about the work for their own records of each child's progress. For some subjects it can be helpful to have a loose-leaf file with a page for each child, to which you add comments as you make observations or mark work. It may also be possible to use a database for recording children's progress which teachers can add to as they assess children.

Where practical work is involved, as in technology, art, physical education and music, teachers need to have a system for observing children, perhaps looking at the progress of a small number in each lesson and recording the findings. In technology there may be a case for photographing finished work as a record. In art, especially with the younger children, teachers might look for stages of development in the drawing of a figure, for example, or the stage where children recognise that the sky and the earth join, as well as the materials children use and the skill with which they handle them. Individual portfolios of work provide useful information about children's development and skill.

Reports to parents

Teachers' records provide the basis for reports to parents. The Qualifications and Curriculum Authority states that reports to parents should include the following.

- Brief comments on the child's progress in each subject and activity studied as part of the school curriculum. These should highlight strengths and development needs.
- The child's general progress.
- Arrangements for the parents to discuss the report at the school.
- Total number of sessions (half-days) since the child's last report or since the child entered the school, whichever is later, and the percentage missed through unauthorised absence. (1999:32)

In Year 6 the school must include SATs results, a statement that the levels have been arrived at by statutory assessment, a statement where the assessment regulations have been disapplied, comparative information about the attainments of children of the same age in the school, and comparative information about the attainment of children of the same age nationally. The QCA document also suggests that parents will want to know how a child is now performing compared with his or her previous performance, his or her strengths and achievements, areas for development and improvement, how parents can help and whether the child is happy, settled and behaving well. It states:

> It is important not to obscure low achievement or under-achievement by the use of faint praise or avoiding mention of the problem. Reports should give an accurate picture of current attainment. They can then be used to involve the child in setting clear, achievable and time-related targets for his or her learning. (1999:53)

Evaluating the effects of change

You also need to be concerned to evaluate the effectiveness or otherwise of any changes which you have agreed with your colleagues. Ideally, evaluation should be considered when the change is planned so that everyone knows that after an agreed period there will be an assessment of how well the change has gone. It is also a good idea to agree in advance the criteria by which success will be judged since this will have an effect on the way the change is carried out.

CASE STUDY

The teachers at New Hampton Junior School decided that they would introduce a new scheme of work for some aspects of English in the junior department of the school, which would involve children in working together at first in pairs and later in small groups, studying different texts and drawing conclusions from them. They spent a lot of time working out how they would do this, the sorts of questions which the children might be asked to look at, and the way that groups would be formed, initially by pairs who had worked together joining with another pair to make a group. There were two classes in each year group, and teachers decided that they would eventually structure groups so that they contained children of varying ability in one class in each year and group by ability in the other. This gave a variety of different contexts which might be studied.

They decided that they would assess the effect of this programme after a term. This would involve asking the children to complete a questionnaire about how they felt about group work and finding a way to assess what had been learned. Children's groups were to be asked to develop a group report on their findings about each text they had studied, and these provided information about what they appeared to have learned. It was also suggested that teachers might talk with a sample group of children in the parallel class to get further information about what the children felt they had learned and what they liked and disliked about the group work. They would also compare the results from the different organisations that had been adopted.

Elizabeth, the subject leader for English, collected information from all these exercises and interviewed all the teachers to get their impressions about how the work had gone. Overall, teachers felt that the children had learned a good deal from the exercise, and the teachers of the classes with mixed ability groups felt that the less able children had benefited from this organisation. The less able groups in the ability grouped classes did not do so well and the groups tended to be mainly boys. The children themselves were generally enthusiastic. They felt that they had learned a good deal and liked having the opportunity to talk through their ideas with others.

Continuity and progression

As subject leader you need to be concerned that there is continuity as children move through the school and that each teacher builds on what has gone before. This should be partly taken care of through the scheme of work. Children's records ought also to provide useful information for the next teacher, and teachers need to be encouraged to talk to each other about the children who are transferring from one class to the next. It is important that there is not only continuity but progression as children grow older. For example, do the ways in which individual teachers deal with Christmas each year represent a progression in learning for the children or merely a repeat of the Christmas story? Does the work in science help children to develop more scientific ways of thinking as they grow older? Are teachers aware of what constitutes progression in your subject?

QUESTIONS FOR CONSIDERATION

1 Have we a clear policy on assessing and evaluating children's work and progress in the subject?

2 Have we agreed ways of recording children's progress? Could we profitably make more use of computers?

3 Have we agreed ways of marking children's work (in subjects where this is applicable) or agreed ways of making assessments in practical subjects?

4 How well are colleagues managing end of Key Stage assessments?

5 Is there good continuity in my subject as children move through the school?

6 How do I evaluate work in my subject overall?

7 How do I share my findings with colleagues?

8 Are any groups of children under-performing? If so, what should we do about this?

9 Are children with special needs making good progress?

10 Are the most able children performing as well as they should be? Have we a system for monitoring their progress?

CHAPTER 13

Providing for all children

Every teacher in a primary school has to deal with children of a wide range of ability. There will be those who make very slow progress and those who race ahead. There may be children with specific disabilities such as poor sight or hearing or a physical disability. There will be children who pose problems because of their behaviour. There may be differences between the performance of boys and girls. There may also be children from ethnic minorities or other foreign nationals for whom English is a second language who may or may not have other learning difficulties. There will be children from a variety of home backgrounds and different social classes. There may be some traveller children only in the school for a short time. Somehow the teacher has to work so that all these children learn and make progress, and the subject leader needs to take all these children into account.

It will be important to ensure that teachers hold high expectations of all children. Research suggests that black Caribbean children, boys in particular, start school doing quite well but do not make good progress. One element in this is that teachers hold low expectations of them. There is also evidence to suggest that boys are generally better at mathematics and science, and girls at language work. You need to check whether this is the case in your school and consider what should be done to enable both boys and girls to achieve in both areas. It is worth discussing the effect of teacher and parent expectations and, when observing teachers at work, noticing if they demonstrate expectations of children which will affect how the children perform.

Britain is now a multicultural and multiracial society and each child's education needs to take account of this and reflect this diversity. Collett quotes the philosophy of one school:

> To develop in every child a critical understanding and respect, both of their own cultural background and the cultural background of their neighbours so that:
>
> - children may be helped to make sense of themselves with particular reference to the culture of which they are a part;
> - children may be helped to decide what kind of person they wish to grow into;
> - children are better equipped to become responsible members of their community, respectful of the views and cultural background of their neighbours. (1994:108)

As subject leader you need to consider what contribution your subject has to make to this development, which is important whether or not the school contains pupils with a variety of backgrounds. It will be particularly important in religious education to help children to develop a respect for all religions, using the experience of any children from different religions wherever possible. In geography and history, knowledge of the countries from which the present population of Britain have come should enable children to empathise with other cultures. In art there may be opportunities to look at the artefacts of other societies. In English there may not only be children for whom English is a foreign language, but also children who do not speak standard English at home. This poses a particular problem for the teacher who has to encourage such children to learn to use standard forms of the language because this will be useful to them in later life, but to do this without denigrating the way they speak at home and among friends. It is similarly important to show children with a home language other than English that their experience is interesting and valued, perhaps asking them to tell others how they say particular things in their home language.

A major consideration for you as a subject leader is the provision for the most and least able children as it affects work in your subject. Dean suggests that a school which provides well for all children is likely to have some or all of the following characteristics:

- A vision of what might be that is shared by staff and governors which is used to develop goals for practice.
- A head teacher and staff who care about children as individuals and are concerned with the development of all of them, whatever their background and ability.
- A head teacher and governing body who are committed to making provision for those with special needs including the exceptionally able and who seek to make as good a provision as they can for these children and do all they can to help and support the teachers concerned.
- A teaching staff in which all teachers see it as a professional challenge to provide for the learning of all the children in their care and to solve the problems that this involves. They therefore share ideas and materials and help each other with problems, are sensitive to children's needs and properly encouraging of progress. They have high expectations of children and are optimistic that all pupils can succeed.
- A teaching staff in which at least one member is expert in special needs and is able to act as adviser to other colleagues, offering ideas about problems and resources and keeping up to date with new developments and to whom teachers can turn readily for advice and guidance.

- An overall policy coordinating provision which ensures that children with special needs are identified, that their progress is monitored and recorded, that resources are available, that teachers are aware of the school programme for dealing with this area of work and that external agencies and resources are fully used, i.e. that the Code of Practice is implemented.
- A practice of assessing individual children carefully, of working diagnostically whenever possible and then matching the programme to the needs of the child. (1996:10)

The *Special Educational Needs Code of Practice* sets out the following principles:

- a child with special educational needs should have their needs met;
- the special educational needs of children will normally be met in mainstream schools or settings;
- the views of the child should be sought and taken into account;
- parents have a vital role to play in supporting their child's education;
- children with special educational needs should be offered full access to a broad, balanced and relevant curriculum, including an appropriate curriculum for the foundation stage and the National Curriculum. (DfES 2001:7)

The *Code of Practice* defines special educational needs as follows:

Children have special educational needs if they have a *learning difficulty* which calls for *special educational provision* to be made for them.

Children have a learning difficulty if they:

a) have a significantly greater difficulty in learning than the majority of children of the same age; or
b) have a disability which prevents or hinders them from making use of educational facilities of a kind generally provided for children of the same age in schools within the area of the local education authority. (DfES 2001:6)

If we regard exceptional ability as a special need we will be looking for children with some of the following characteristics:

- at least one area of outstanding ability, whether very advanced attainment, ideas, interests or skills;
- the ability to learn easily and quickly and the ability to handle complex information;
- with a wide range of interests and hobbies;
- superiority compared with other children in the age group in quality and quantity of vocabulary;

- the ability to work independently, showing perseverance and good attention;
- alertness and quick response to new ideas;
- unusual imagination and originality;
- be a very advanced or rapid reader who may have learned to read early;
- may be socially mature;
- may have an outstanding sense of humour.

As a subject leader you need to be concerned not only with children who fail to make progress in literacy and numeracy but also in the knowledge and skills which affect your subject. In the case of subjects like history and geography, literacy skills are important, but in a subject like technology manual skills and creative ability are needed. In physical education children may or may not have good physical skills. In music a child may or may not have a musical ear. In art children develop through various stages and some children may develop much more slowly than others. You need to be concerned with the progress children make in your subject. You also need to be concerned with those children who show exceptional ability in your subject and in all these cases you need to be ready to help your colleagues to make suitable provision.

In this work you need to work closely with the Special Educational Needs Coordinator (SENCO) who may also be regarded as a subject leader. The *Special Educational Needs Code of Practice* defines the responsibilities of the SENCO as follows:

- overseeing the day-to-day operation of the school's SEN policy;
- coordinating provision for children with special educational needs;
- liaising with and advising fellow teachers;
- managing learning support assistants;
- overseeing the records of all children with special educational needs;
- liaising with parents of children with special educational needs;
- contributing to the in-service training of staff;
- liaising with external services including the LEA's support and educational psychology services, health and social services, and voluntary bodies. (DfES 2001:50)

The SENCO is also responsible for keeping a register of children with special educational needs and ensuring that an Individual Education Plan (IEP) is provided for each child and discussed with the class teacher. He or she is also responsible for any Learning Support Assistants the school employs, providing training for them and ensuring that their services are well used. As a subject leader you need to consider and talk with your colleagues about the signs of exceptional ability in your subject as well as helping them to find ways of providing for such children. Wallace suggests that the needs of the very able spring from three main sources:

> **CASE STUDY**
>
> Sheila was the SENCO for a one-form entry primary school. She taught a Year 4 class with an afternoon a week clear to support special educational needs work across the school. She had three children with special needs in her class, and a Learning Support Assistant worked with her for part of the week to provide help for these children.
>
> In working with her class, she noticed that she had two children who were nearly always ahead of everyone else. Their hands were the first to go up in answer to questions. Their written work was nearly always of a high quality and there was evidence that they read widely. Her interest in children with special needs made her extra conscious of the need to provide for some children as individuals and she started to make Individual Education Plans involving these two children. This worked well and it occurred to her that it might be a good idea to do this throughout the school.
>
> After a good deal of thought about what it might involve in work for her and other people, she put the idea to colleagues that they might treat very able children as also having special needs, including any who had specific talents such as musical or artistic ability or were very creative. She would keep a register of them and work with each teacher and each of the children concerned to develop an Individual Education Plan.
>
> The staff thought this over and came to the conclusion that it was a good idea. They talked for a while about how they should recognise very able children. Some were immediately evident but some might not show their ability at an early stage, especially if they didn't want to seem different from their friends. Would a teacher recognise exceptional ability in music, for example if he or she was not very musical? This discussion turned out to be quite profitable in helping to make everyone more aware of the signs of exceptional ability.
>
> They went on to suggest that the school might make some additional special provision for such children – perhaps an after-school club or an opportunity for a group of very able children to come together to work at a project if this could be arranged. It would also be helpful to teachers to discuss how they were providing for such children.
>
> The plans were put into action and resulted in some very interesting work.

1. *A feeling of being different:* 'I am the loneliest person in the world. I'm inventing things now but I have to wait until I'm grown up because no one will listen to me' (able child).
2. *The burden of high sensitivity:* Many very able children are acutely sensitive to the world around them; they have a precocious understanding of adult issues and a premature intellectual awareness of problems without the emotional maturity to cope with them.
3. *Exceptional learning ability:* The problem for them is that the class is too slow. (1983:10)

She goes on to say:

> The teacher of very able children needs the maturity to accept a child with possibly a higher potential than herself, who will sometimes challenge and even threaten the teacher's knowledge and feeling of security. (1983:16)

She suggests that the teacher needs to be a co-learner exploring new ideas with the child who needs a different pace and depth of experience from other children. Such children may be careless and untidy writers and it is important for the teacher to listen carefully to what the child has to say, to the quality of thinking and the development of ideas. How does he or she approach problems?

As subject leader you also need to be aware of any differences there may be in the interests and achievements of boys and girls. Some subjects have greater appeal to one or the other. Boys tend to do better in science and mathematics and girls in language work. Is this true in your school? Do you and your colleagues need to do anything to improve the performance of any one group?

QUESTIONS FOR CONSIDERATION

1 Do any children pose problems in my subject because they have a disability?

2 Does teaching in my subject contribute in any way to multicultural education?

3 What problems for teachers of my subject are posed by children for whom English is a second language? Can I do anything to help?

4 How do we deal with children who do not speak standard English at home?

5 What is the nature of learning difficulties in my subject? How should we assess and diagnose these difficulties?

6 What provision should we make for children with learning difficulties in my subject?

7 What sorts of evidence will suggest to a teacher that a child has exceptional ability in my subject?

8 What sorts of provision should we make for children with exceptional ability?

9 Do we expect too little of black children, particularly boys? What can we do about it?

10 How do the performances of boys and girls compare? Is there a need to make special provision for one or the other?

CHAPTER 14

Getting organised

Being a subject leader in a primary school is a demanding role. Primary schoolteachers have very little time available for leadership roles and it is important that you use your time and energy as effectively as possible.

Self-evaluation

It is a good idea to start with self-evaluation. The National Standards for Subject Leaders gives the following list of the knowledge and understanding a subject leader needs. You can assess yourself against this list and consider the implications of your findings for your own professional development.

Subject leaders should have knowledge and understanding of:

1. their school's aims, priorities, targets and action plans;
2. the relationship of the subject to the curriculum as a whole;
3. any statutory curriculum requirements for the subject and requirements for assessment, recording and reporting of pupils' attainment and progress;
4. the characteristics of high quality teaching in the subject and the main strategies for improving and sustaining high standards of teaching, learning and achievement for all pupils;
5. how evidence from relevant research and inspection evidence and local, national and international standards of achievement in the subject can be used to inform expectations, targets and teaching approaches;
6. how to use comparative data, together with information about pupils' prior attainment, to establish benchmarks and set targets for improvement;
7. how to develop pupils' literacy, numeracy and information technology skills through the subject;
8. how teaching the subject can promote pupils' spiritual, moral, social, cultural, mental and physical development;
9. management, including employment law, equal opportunities legislation, personnel, external relations, finance and change;
10. how teaching the subject can help to prepare pupils for the opportunities, responsibilities and experiences of adult life;
11. the current use and future potential of information and communications

technology to aid teaching and learning of the subject, and to assist with subject management;

12. the role of school governance and how it can contribute to the work of the subject leader;
13. the implications of information and guidance documents from LEAs, the DfES, WOED and other national bodies and associations;
14. the implications of the Code of Practice for Special Educational Needs for teaching and learning in the subject;
15. health and safety requirements, including where to obtain expert advice.

You also need to look at the way you work with colleagues and children and seek feedback from other people about the way they see your work. Do you create trust by acting reliably, fairly and consistently? Do you communicate effectively with your colleagues, the head teacher and the children? Do you share objectives for your subject with the rest of the staff? Do you listen to other people's ideas and show that you respect and value them? Do you seek out children's views and listen to what they have to say about work in your subject? How good are you at analysing and solving problems? Do you seek out information so that you really know what is going on? Are you systematic in collecting information? How well do you manage conflict? Are you sufficiently flexible? Can you change and adapt to changing circumstances?

The school's programme of performance management should help you to look critically at your work as a subject leader as well as at your role as a classroom teacher. Your interview with the head teacher or other manager should give you feedback on your work. It is important to listen carefully to what is being said without being defensive, even if you feel that the view being stated is inaccurate. The fact that someone sees your work in this light is something to take note of so that you can work to change the view being expressed. Ask questions so that you are really clear about the message.

An important outcome of your self-evaluation performance management review and feedback from colleagues is a clarification of your professional development needs. Are there areas of your work where you feel less than fully competent? Do you need to know more about some aspects? Are you well acquainted with developments in your subject? Does the feedback you are getting suggest any areas in which you need to learn more? You then need to think about the ways in which you can meet your own needs, perhaps by seeking out suitable courses, by reading, by action research (see Chapter 16) or by visiting other schools.

Personal organisation

You need to be well organised to be a good subject leader. The demands of the role are considerable and there is very little time to do all that is necessary. You need to consider the following practices:

- Make long-term plans, for the year and for the term, and record in your diary and on a year or term planner all deadlines and commitments.
- Make a weekly action plan and then prioritise your actions, taking account of importance and urgency.
- Make a daily 'to do' list, highlighting the urgent tasks. Try to make a regular time for dealing with routine matters each day. Get to school early if you can and deal with outstanding tasks before school begins.
- Have a clear filing system and mark each item that you file with the number of the file it goes into so that you can find it again and replace it without too much thought. Aim to handle each piece of paper only once before filing it or deciding what else to do with it and then throw away what is not important.
- Use your computer as much as possible and develop your skills so that you make the maximum use of ICT.
- Make sure that you communicate adequately with your colleagues. Ensure that they know your plans for the subject. Meetings should have agendas well in advance and minutes after the meetings which detail the actions which are to be taken and by whom.

As subject leader you need to keep a number of documents, filed so that they are easily available. These might well include:

- your job description;
- the Teacher Training Agency paper – the National Standards for Subject Leaders;
- any school policy statements and guidelines relevant to your role;
- any subject policy statements;
- the scheme of work for your subject;
- the school development plan and your subject development plan;
- notes of the outcome of your performance management interviews;
- a list of the resources available for your subject with a note of where they are stored and how they can be accessed;
- notes of support offered to colleagues;
- notes of any monitoring of work undertaken;
- minutes and notes of meetings.

The problem of time

Bell and Ritchie list the following problems of time for subject leaders:

- it is not possible to carry out every aspect of the job and some tasks are left undone;
- too much of the time talking to colleagues ends up being a snatched two- or three-minute conversation in the corridor or on playground duty and only rarely a sustained conversation;
- increasingly subject leaders have curriculum management time but little of it, if any, is during the school day to work alongside colleagues;
- much of the work has to be done at home in the evening, if tasks are to be completed;
- time to carry out tasks is not guaranteed so it is difficult to plan ahead;
- there is a constant conflict of responsibilities, particularly with the demands of being a class teacher and meeting requests from children. (1999:134)

They go on to suggest that subject leaders should evaluate the way they use their time, asking the following questions:

1. What am I trying to achieve in terms of the whole school, my responsibilities as subject leader and in other aspects of my life?
2. What do I spend my time doing and what do I need time for?
3. What are my priorities and what do I need to do to meet these?
4. What are the things that stop me carrying out the tasks identified as priorities?
5. What strategies can I implement in order to use my time more effectively and efficiently?

It is helpful to consider the way you use your working day. You have little control over the best part of your working day when you will be teaching, but it is worth considering what is your best time for work that requires careful thought and planning to make full use of such times when they occur. Don't put off doing things which you don't like doing more than you can help. Try to set aside time for professional reading. It is also worth considering whether there is any possibility of delegating some tasks – it may be possible to get a teaching assistant or a volunteer helper to undertake tasks like looking after resources or even helping you to analyse the results of a survey.

Stress

Teaching is a stressful occupation and the subject leadership role can add to the stress. You may find yourself stressed because of not having enough time to do things as well as you would like. Demands from colleagues may be stressful, especially if you feel that your relationships with certain people are not sufficiently positive. This will be especially true if your relationship with your head teacher is not a positive one. The workload may seem too heavy and you may feel that your contribution to the work of the school is insufficiently valued. You may also have a stressful situation of some kind at home which makes the stress in school seem more acute.

It is important that you recognise that you are stressed and to look for ways of managing your role so that the stress is eased. Are you doing anything which isn't absolutely necessary? Is there anyone you can talk to about the way you are feeling who might help with suggestions about better management of time? Can you break down the tasks you have to do into more manageable stages? Are you too easily persuaded to take on extra tasks? Can you say 'No' when necessary? Is there any possibility of delegating some of your work? It is a good idea to make a point of tackling the most difficult tasks early in the day when you can. Try rewarding yourself for finishing a task sometimes. Make sure you get enough sleep – tiredness is stressful.

CASE STUDY

Kathryn was subject leader for mathematics and had held the post for nearly a year. She had worked with colleagues to develop a new scheme of work and a development plan for the subject but was conscious that not all was going according to plan. Not everyone went along with the development plan and the newly qualified teacher in the school was having considerable difficulty in the subject. Her own class was a demanding one with a small number of difficult children, some of whom had learning difficulties. Kathryn also felt under pressure from home where she had two daughters now in secondary school, one of whom was dyslexic. She felt that school work was never done. To add to the pressure the school had just received notice of a pending OFSTED inspection.

When her performance review interview came round, Geoff, her head teacher, started by saying that he had noticed that she seemed to be tired and worried and no longer the lively teacher she had been before she took on the subject leadership role, although he felt that she had done a very good job as subject leader to date. She agreed that she felt stressed and they went on to discuss what might be done to relieve the pressure.

Geoff offered to provide supply cover for three half-days to enable her to see other teachers at work. He also suggested that she might make more use of the teaching assistants and parent volunteers in looking after resources. He thought it might be a good idea for her to keep a diary of how she used her time on tasks related to the subject leadership role. This would enable her to check whether she was using time to the best advantage. They also discussed the possibility of her getting to school half an hour earlier in the morning if this was possible. This would give her some time before school began to deal with problems likely to arise during the day and would give her a bit of time to prepare for the OFSTED inspection. They talked about possible approaches to the teachers who were not going along with the development plan. Overall, Kathryn felt that Geoff had been very supportive and encouraging and was happy to try out the ideas that he was suggesting.

Kemp and Nathan quote the following comments made by teachers about good team leaders:

- She really does listen to what we have to say.
- He works hard, and expects the same from us.
- She is good about thanking you for what you do – it's always nice to feel appreciated for things you have done really well.
- If she feels that you are not doing something as well as you should, then she will say so – she's firm but fair.
- He's not afraid to make difficult decisions.
- There's no doubt who is the leader of the teachers, but we are all made to feel that we are contributing. (1989:114)

Networking

As a subject leader you need to be in touch with what is happening in the subject locally and nationally. Your knowledge of the subject needs to be continually developing if you are to lead your colleagues in their work. There are many sources of information available to you and you need to use any opportunities you can to widen your knowledge and increase your skill.

Most subjects have a national organisation for teachers which organises conferences and courses and provides papers on developments in the subject. It is a good idea to belong to a subject organisation and to make use of the services it offers to help you to keep informed. Subject organisations are not only for secondary schoolteachers, and primary schoolteachers will be welcomed.

It is also a good idea to be in touch with the subject teachers in your local secondary school or schools to which your children transfer. This will be a valuable source of information about developments in the subject and it will be helpful to you and your colleagues to know the kind of teaching which your children will receive when they transfer to secondary education. It is also helpful to know something about the kinds of records of children which the secondary school department would find helpful. If you can get time to visit the secondary school and see some of the staff in action, this is very helpful. Your secondary colleagues may be knowledgeable about aspects of the subject which you want to develop

It is similarly valuable for infant or first school subject leaders to be in touch with their junior or middle school colleagues to find out what the children will be doing when they transfer. Junior or middle schoolteachers also need to be in touch with their infant or first school colleagues so that they know what the children have done when they join the junior or middle school.

There is also value in keeping in touch with other primary schools and it is useful if subject leaders for particular subjects can meet from time to time. It is helpful if a local adviser can organise such groups and arrange for subject leaders to exchange information about the work in their schools, perhaps meeting in a different school each time so that colleagues can look at work there.

Such a group may develop from a teachers' course where those concerned want to go on meeting after the course is over to exchange information and ideas.

Another source of information comes from reading. You would be wise to read the educational press regularly as well as read books about your subject and ways of teaching it. You can then perhaps feed back some of the material you have gleaned from your reading to colleagues.

Subject leaders need to take any opportunity that offers to inform parents and governors about work in their subject. Many schools provide slots in governors' meetings from presentations by subject leaders so that governors know what is being taught in the school. You may also have the chance to talk a group of parents, telling them about the work you and your colleagues are doing and suggesting ways in which they can help.

QUESTIONS FOR CONSIDERATION

1 How do I measure up against the list of skills and knowledge given in the National Standards for Subject Leaders?

2 Is there any area of my work for which I feel I need further training?

3 How well do I work with my colleagues? Do they trust me? Do they come to me for help?

4 Do I make satisfactory long- and short-term plans?

5 Do I make a daily 'to do' list highlighting the urgent tasks?

6 Have I an effective filing system? Do I use it well?

7 Do I make the maximum use of ICT?

8 Do I communicate adequately with my colleagues?

9 Is my documentation up to date?

10 How well do I use the time I have available for my subject leader role?

11 Do I suffer from stress? If so, what can I do about it?

12 Do I make enough use of networks of contacts to inform my work as subject leader?

CHAPTER 15

Working with support staff

All schools are now likely to have some help from a variety of support staff. These will include administrative and clerical staff, school meals staff, lunchtime supervisors, technicians as well as support staff (often called Teaching Assistants or Learning Support Assistants) who work alongside teachers in the classroom. As subject leader you need to ensure that support staff involved with the teaching of your subject are well used.

The DfES website on developing the role of school support staff suggests that teachers spend about 20 per cent of their time on non-teaching tasks which could equally well be done by other staff. If this provision were available then there would be:

- more time for high quality and more individualised lesson planning, preparation and pupil assessment;
- relief from any bureaucracy that gets in the way of what matters most in teaching and learning and raising standards of pupil achievement;
- extra support inside and outside the classroom with new school support staff filling roles at every level in the school so that teachers can focus on teaching.

Government proposals for increasing the number of teaching assistants in schools suggest that primary schoolteachers should not do the following;

- Collect money (for lunches, trips etc.).
- Chase absent pupils.
- Photocopy in bulk.
- Type.
- Produce standard letters.
- Compile class lists.
- Keep records and do filing.
- Make classroom displays.
- Collate parts of pupil reports together.
- Organise cover for absent staff.
- Commission new ICT equipment.
- Order supplies and equipment.
- Stocktake.
- Catalogue, prepare, issue and maintain equipment and materials.
- Take minutes at meetings.

- Manage pupil data.
- Input pupil data.

Mortimore *et al.* suggest that schools might make an audit of current practices looking at the following questions:

- What does each teacher currently do?
- What new demands/tasks have been added to their roles?
- What proportion of their time is spent on each task?
- What is the cost of this time?
- What aspects of the teacher's role are suffering as a result of added demands?
- What aspects of the teacher's current role, which are related directly to their professional and pedagogic responsibilities, could be delegated to another person who is not a teacher?
- Could the work be organised so as to benefit from the complementary skills of current associate staff? (1994:210)

Support staff may bring many skills and areas of knowledge to a school. While a school may be looking for specific skills to complement those of the teaching staff, it is also worth exploring whether an individual has any additional skills or interests which would be valuable to the children. It is also worth while to consider what such staff might offer if given additional training in particular areas of work. Support assistants may undertake any of the tasks listed above that teachers should not be required to do. They may also undertake reading and mathematical activities and record children's progress, play learning games with children, work with groups of children on tasks agreed with the teacher, manage ICT, support children with special needs, do extension work with very able children, put up displays, organise and maintain resource collections, and many other things. As subject leader you need to consider ways in which support staff could help in the teaching of your subject. Different teachers and different assistants will have ideas about this and it may be a good idea to discuss them together so that everyone is using the assistance available as well as possible.

It is important for teachers and support staff to consider where the boundaries lie between them. These will vary according to the particular skills a support assistant brings to the task. In some situations, the assistant may be more knowledgeable than the teacher and may need the freedom to use his or her knowledge and skills. At the same time, the overall responsibility for what happens in the classroom is the teacher's and this needs to be clear. This will be particularly relevant in terms of the assistant's involvement in discipline. It should be clear that any bad behaviour should be reported to the teacher who should deal with it.

Support staff usually welcome training which enables them to work more effectively. Discussion about the ways in which support staff can contribute to the teaching of your subject is helpful and you may want to provide some in-service training about the subject area and the way they can best contribute. The school may also run more general training for them to which you may be able to contribute.

CASE STUDY

Janice was the SENCO for her primary school. She had been in post for six months and had been able to assess a number of children with special needs over this period. Several of them were referred on to the local authority as needing Statements and after appropriate testing Statements were issued. As a result of this three Learning Support Assistants had been appointed to help these children and were to take up their posts in the autumn term.

Janice arranged a two-day course for them at the end of the summer holidays so that they could be prepared to start work in the classroom as soon as term began. It had been agreed with the class teachers that the LSAs would help other children with difficulties as well as those with Statements, so that no child would feel singled out.

The course started with information about the way the school taught reading and mathematics, so that the LSAs could fit in with the work the class teachers were doing. Janice showed them the materials teachers were using and described the way in which each teacher was trying to provide for children with special needs. She then spent time individually with each person telling her about the children she was likely to be working with. She showed them the psychologist's report for each child and the comments that the class teacher had made and her own assessment and test results so that they were really in the picture.

The school may also make some use of volunteers. These may be parents or governors or people who live locally who are prepared to give some time to help the school. It will be important to maintain a clear distinction between the tasks that volunteers and paid support staff are asked to do. Some, like the support staff, will have skills and knowledge which can be useful. Some may undertake a mentoring role with children who need extra attention. They may be used to hear reading – a different role from that of the assistant who carries out reading activities with children. You may want to arrange some training for volunteers as well as support staff.

Both support staff and volunteers need to be given information about the school when they first work there. It is a good idea to have a file of information for them, giving a plan of the school and basic facts such as any arrangements for parking, lunch arrangements, the school's expectations in terms of the tasks they might be asked to do, what to do about bad behaviour, and the confidentiality needed in the role.

QUESTIONS FOR CONSIDERATION

1   What use do I need to make of support staff to help in the teaching of my subject?

2   Is there a place for volunteers in the teaching of my subject?

3   Are there any tasks I do which could be done by support staff or volunteers?

4   Have any of the support staff or volunteers skills or knowledge which could be particularly useful in the teaching of my subject?

5   Do support staff or volunteers need any training to enable them to work more effectively in the classroom?

6   Are there any difficulties arising because the boundaries between teachers and support staff are not clear?

7   What arrangements have we made as a school for inducting new support staff and volunteers?

CHAPTER 16

Action research

As a subject leader you are responsible both for encouraging the professional development of your colleagues and for raising the levels of pupil achievement in your subject. Action research offers a way of doing both these things which is non-threatening to teachers. It also gives you a chance to monitor work in your subject in a way which enhances, rather than diminishes teacher self-esteem. It can lead to the staff becoming a self-critical and reflective community in which people support each other in developing their work. Busher and Harris suggest that action research is 'likely to promote effective social cohesion in a subject area team and coherent and effective team approaches to improving practice' (2000:viii).

Lieberman and Miller write of the learning school as one that fosters learning on five levels:

1. It facilitates and maximises the learning of all students.
2. It enables the teachers to be continuing learners themselves.
3. It encourages teachers to learn together and from one another in collaboration.
4. It is a learning environment that is both responsive and adaptive to internal and external pressures.
5. It is an institution in which the principal is the leading learner and is able to model learning behaviour for teachers and students alike. (1991:124)

As subject leader you need to contribute to the possibility of your school becoming a learning school in which everybody is committed to learning. Action research is one way to encourage this.

A good way to start action research projects is to gather together a small group of colleagues interested in finding new ways of working. A group of about four is ideal because it gives enough time for each person's contribution to be carefully considered and suggestions made. Ask each person to come to a meeting prepared to describe to the others an area of work in which he or she would like to tackle a problem or improve children's achievement. The group then suggests ways of improving the situation described and goes on to make plans for each member, considering the information which should be assembled about the current situation, exactly what might be done and how, and also how judgements will be made about the success of the experiment.

Simmons, in a paper presented at a teacher's conference in Denver, describes the changes which occurred in participants in action research:

> They acquired new knowledge of effective teaching and schooling; they improved in their level of cognitive development; they changed in their attitudes towards themselves as teachers; they developed new patterns of communication and collegiality; they developed new theories of their work as classroom teachers; they changed their classroom practice. (1985)

Other researchers have found teachers involved in action research more self-assured, more able to cope with threats to their self-esteem and more able to accept observation of teaching by someone else as a valuable contribution to development.

There would appear to be a number of steps in setting up an action research project:

1. Identify the area or problem in detail in terms of what you want to improve.
2. Collect data about the area or problem. This might include evidence from observing children, from considering children's work and from discussion with them, evidence from another person's observation of work in your classroom, test results or any other evidence which occurs to you.
3. Analyse the data and define the problem in more detail. Your original idea may need to be revised as you find out more about the issue. Avoid selecting an issue you can do nothing about.
4. Define the outcome you want to achieve in terms of children's achievement or behaviour.
5. Plan a programme of action to achieve this outcome. This should include a revised statement of the general idea and a statement of the factors you are thinking of changing. Consider the resources you will need.
6. Plan the way in which you will monitor and evaluate what has happened. Make sure that what you plan will provide evidence of unintended effects as well those which you expect.
7. Implement the programme.
8. Monitor and evaluate the effects of the programme and the changes that have taken place.

In starting a programme of action research you need to decide whether a particular investigation is to be focused or exploratory and open-ended. Sometimes you will have very definite idea of what you want to do and sometimes a particular problem will be rather vague and will need a good deal of investigation before you can gradually focus on what you want to do and are able to define your area of research clearly. You need to think about the information you require, where you can find it and how you can best collect it.

Some of the following kinds of evidence may be used to contribute to your plan of action and to assess whether your plan has worked:

- Diaries can be kept by you or by the children giving personal accounts of observations, feelings, ideas, reflections and explanations. An advantage of both children and teacher keeping diaries is that the accounts can be compared. You would be wise to keep a diary of the progress of any study, making notes each day of what has happened.
- Tape recordings and transcripts. Audio-tape can be very useful in recording what you and the children say. Video-tape is also very useful but needs another person to record.
- Involving an observer. An observer well briefed by the teacher can be very valuable in giving an independent view of the situation. It is helpful if the observer makes notes of what he or she sees and what is happening and makes these available to the teacher concerned. When observations are received from three sources, such as the children, the teacher and an observer, this is known as triangulation and it is a valuable way of getting and being able to compare a variety of views of a situation, looking at where they agree and where they differ.
- Questionnaires for the children can be helpful in helping them to express their views, perhaps asking them whether they agree or disagree with certain statements and providing them with an opportunity to say what they found helpful, enjoyable or difficult.

CASE STUDY

Clare was the subject leader for English in a two-form entry junior school and had a Year 6 class herself. She was keen on the idea of action research and had discussed it with a number of colleagues. Clare wanted to improve her children's ability to write stories. She collected a number of stories they had written and discussed them with a colleague. They agreed that they were rather dull and lacking in local colour in spite of her effort to make them more interesting.

Clare then set out to think about what would make a story more interesting. She concluded that there was a need to set the scene in some detail so that the reader could picture it and then to introduce the characters and describe them before going on to write about the plot of the story. She talked with the children about descriptions of places and people and they searched out good descriptions in books and talked about them. She spent some time going over the writing of speech, which the children tended to avoid because they were afraid to make mistakes in punctuation.

She then decided that each child would write a story which would be marked in the first place by the child next to him or her in a similar way to the way the teacher would have marked it. This would involve marking mistakes in an agreed way and writing a comment at the end praising what was good and suggesting improvements. Clare spent some time with the class going over the criteria for a good story – descriptions of setting, characters and plot, reporting of speech by the characters, interesting sentences with good use of adjectives and adverbs, and so on, and explaining that the markers needed to bear these points in mind when marking.

The stories were finished for homework and time was set aside the following day for the marking to take place. When it was completed she spent some time discussing with the children how they felt about it and what they felt they had learned, and she also asked them to write about why they felt that the experience had been useful. They were generally enthusiastic about this idea and felt that they had learned a good deal about story writing because it had become important to get the marking right.

Clare went over the marking they had done and found that in many cases they had said much the same as she would have said herself. She also asked the teacher of the parallel class to look at the the work and she confirmed Clare's impressions. The next task was to see whether the exercise would result in better stories in the future.

When you have undertaken a piece of action research you need to look critically at what you have done. You then need to think about whether to report your findings to other teachers so that they can learn from your experience. If you have been part of a group in which each member has undertaken some action research this will form a ready-made audience for a report on the findings of each member.

QUESTIONS FOR CONSIDERATION

1 In what areas of work do I want to improve children's learning?

2 Which of these would lend itself to action research?

3 What information do I need to gather? From whom and from where should I gather it?

4 What does the data suggest that I might do?

5 How shall I set about the experiment?

6 Whom should I involve in looking at what happens? What data should I gather? How should I gather it?

7 What conclusions can I draw from the data collected? Are my conclusions valid?

8 What have I and the children learned from the exercise?

9 What conclusions should I share with other people?

10 Where should I go from here?

CHAPTER 17

Dealing with problems

Every subject leader has a number of problems to deal with. When confronting a problem it may help to think through some of the following stages:

- What is the nature of the problem? Whom does it concern? What are the facts about it?
- What are the possible solutions? It may help to have a brainstorming session with a group of colleagues if the problem concerns them too.
- What are the pros and cons of the various alternative solutions? Which ones are actually possible? What would be the side-effects of each one?
- Which solution offers the best likelihood of a good outcome?

You can then start to plan to put the best solution into effect. It is a good idea to think at the same time about how you will evaluate the success or otherwise of your plan.

The problem of finding time for the job

A problem for all subject leaders is that of finding enough time to do the job. You need time to meet and talk with colleagues about work in your subject area, time to observe them in action and look at children's work, time to deal with resources for the subject, time to help colleagues develop their work and time to evaluate what is happening, and much else. Suggestions for dealing with this problem and planning the use of time were given in Chapter 14.

Problems in relationships with colleagues

There may also be problems in dealing with your colleagues. You may have colleagues who do not want to work in ways you are suggesting, who resist new ideas and are generally uncooperative. This may be a particular problem where the staff in question are older and more experienced than you are and feel that you have little to offer them. It may be useful in this case to enlist other experienced staff who are in sympathy with what you are trying to do, asking them to talk to the more resistant colleagues. The balance of views in a meeting may also be supportive and the colleagues who are being resistant may be persuaded by the more positive views of others. There may also be a situation where you can offer new resources to persuade a colleague to go along with a new way of working. You need to be a good listener, ready to explore what someone else sees as a difficulty with a new development and ready to use problem-solving skills and take any opportunity which offers to help a colleague.

At the same time you need to be assertive. Assertiveness was discussed briefly in Chapter 1. Kemp and Nathan suggest that when you are employing assertive behaviour you may act as follows:

1. State your rights – with a straightforward statement that stands up for your rights by stating your needs clearly and reasonably.
2. Ask the other person with a straightforward question designed to clarify where the other person stands, or what he or she wants or needs.
3. Understand both views – show that you do appreciate the other person's view, while at the same time stating your own needs.
4. State the effects of behaviour with a statement that openly explains the adverse effect a person's behaviour is having on you. (1989:128)

In assertive behaviour distinguish between fact and opinion and look for ways to resolve problems.

Another problem is the person who is always complaining. He or she very often picks on things to complain about which you can do very little about. The best way to deal with this is to listen attentively so that the complainer feels that he or she is being taken seriously without appearing to agree and then try to find aspects of the problem which are solvable and about which something can be done.

You may also meet colleagues who appear to be negative about everything you suggest. This is discouraging but the best way to deal with this may be to ask whether the speaker has a better suggestion.

You may also have to deal with conflict. This was discussed in Chapter 6. There may be a conflict with the ideas you want to implement or conflict between other teachers or teachers and assistants which is getting in the way of the work. Conflict should be talked out frankly wherever possible, acknowledging that there are different ways of looking at things and seeking ways forward. Differences of view are valuable and conflict can sometimes be productive in making people think about what they believe and what they are doing.

CASE STUDY

The head teacher of Maybury Junior School had a problem. Marion, a newly qualified teacher and a committed Christian, had told her Year 4 class that Christianity was the only true religion. Unfortunately the class contained three Muslim children and one Jewish child and all their parents had made complaints about this. The head saw Marion and warned her that she must not make or imply such a view again and asked Joanna, the subject leader for religious education, to talk to Marion and explain to her the purpose of religious education and discuss with her how she intended to deal with the parts of the syllabus which dealt with other religions.

Joanna found Marion deeply concerned that she might have to teach children about religions which she believed to be untrue and unready to accept that other people felt as deeply as she did about their beliefs. Joanna explained that religious education was about helping children to understand other faiths, but Marion was adamant that she could not square this kind of teaching with her conscience. After a long discussion they agreed that Marion would continue to teach that part of the syllabus which concerned Christianity, being careful not to treat this as an opportunity to evangelise, and would exchange classes with Joanna who would teach Marion's class about other faiths while Marion taught Joanna's class about Christianity.

Supporting colleagues who are in difficulties

One of the most difficult tasks for people in leadership roles in schools is that of helping teachers who are struggling. A teacher may be identified as having difficulties as a result of an inspection or complaints from parents or from the observations of the head teacher and colleagues. The difficulties may be particularly evident in your subject and you may be asked if you can help. Wragg *et al.* list six criteria of good management practice in dealing with poorly performing staff in schools:

1. the assessment of performance based on evidence, not hearsay;
2. an approach combining support with a determination to secure acceptable improvement;
3. the seeking of innovative solutions, rather than an unbending obduracy which only seeks improved performance in an unchanged job;
4. giving consideration to the dignity of the poor performer, and honourable solutions are sought rather than punitive ones;
5. learning lessons about the prevention of future poor performance rather than accepting poor performance as inevitable;
6. ensuring that the interests of the children are paramount. (2000:41)

Poor performance may include inadequate classroom management and discipline, poor relationships with children, colleagues and parents, inability to help children to achieve. Wragg *et al.* suggested that some incompetent teachers had rigid personalities and unrealistic expectations of children.

> They alienated their pupils by relying too heavily on 'chalk and talk'. They shouted and harangued children, expecting them to sit and listen, regardless of how boring or badly planned the lesson was, and when they failed to do so, the teachers blamed the pupils, rather than blaming their own practice. (2000:47)

Such a teacher poses a difficult problem for the school and for the head teacher in particular, and you, along with other colleagues, may be asked to help in any way you can. It is best if this is part of a programme of help and advice aimed at overcoming some of the difficulties the teacher is experiencing. It will be helpful to have the opportunity to observe what is happening in the classroom. You may then be able to help by discussing work with the teacher, suggesting resources or approaches to the work. You may also be able to help by team teaching with the teacher if time can be found for you to work with him or her. This would require you to plan with the teacher concerned, demonstrating more satisfactory ways of working than those you have observed. It will be important that the plans are really jointly made so that the teacher feels some ownership of what is planned. You also need to think out clearly how you will each work. Your presence may help if the teacher concerned normally has a discipline problem and this may give him or her some leads on how to control the class more effectively.

A different approach may be to plan together, feeding in ideas for a lesson which you will observe. You might agree beforehand the points you will look out for and record, so that you can give some useful feedback after the lesson. It may also be useful for the teacher to observe you teaching, either the teacher's class or your own. Suggest points in advance for the observer to note and discuss them afterwards.

Preparing for OFSTED

Most teachers feel some concern when the school faces an OFSTED inspection. It is always disturbing to feel that judgements are being made about one's work, and this is likely to be the case however experienced and able you are. You can only do your best and hope that the work that is observed goes according to plan. However, you can see that all the evidence the inspectors are likely to look for is in place. Are your policy statements up to date? Is your scheme of work complete, stating aims and meeting the requirements of the National Curriculum? Does it cover work with children of all abilities? Has every teacher a copy of the scheme and do you know how well it is being followed? If you are leading a core subject, how well are children achieving in national tests? How well are children doing when assessed by the National Curriculum levels? What sorts of records of work are teachers keeping? Are the resources for your subject well organised and well used? What are the attitudes of children to the subject? Is homework being used effectively? How do you assess what is happening in your subject?

Bell and Ritchie give the following list of questions which subject leaders might be asked by inspectors:

- What is being achieved in your subject? How do you know? What opportunities do you have for finding out? If you have curriculum management (non-contact) time, how do you use it?
- What are the priorities for development in your subject? How do you contribute to the school development plan? Is there a subject development plan? Do you have an action plan?
- How was the subject's policy developed? Is it subject to review?
- How would you describe your current roles and responsibilities as a coordinator/subject leader? How were you appointed? Do you have subject expertise, or just personal interest in the subject? How was your job description arrived at? Is it published?
- Do you have responsibility for a budget? If so, how do you manage it? What are your priorities for spending at present? What is planned for the future? Have you audited resources recently? Are there any gaps in current resources?
- What in-service training have teachers received recently in the subject? Have you led or are you planning to lead, any in-service training? How do you support your colleagues?
- Have non-teaching staff or parents received any support (training, workshops or talks)?
- Has in-service training had any significant impact on the standards of pupils' work?
- What in-service training have you received as a subject leader, and what impact has it had?
- How do you assess and keep records of work covered, pupils' achievements and progress? How is this information reported to parents and others?
- Are there any specific arrangements to support pupils with special needs in your subject?
- Are there any developments in your subject about which you are

particularly pleased? Are there any constraints on developments in your subject? (1999:154)

QUESTIONS FOR CONSIDERATION

1 What problems am I meeting as a subject leader?

2 Is finding time for the work a problem? If so, what am I doing about it?

3 Have I any particular problems in relationships with colleagues? Are any of my colleagues resistant to my attempts to lead the work?

4 How well do I deal with conflict? Am I sufficiently assertive?

5 Am I giving sufficient support to any newly qualified teachers or teachers new to the staff?

6 Are any of my colleagues struggling with my subject? What can I do to help?

7 Am I prepared for an OFSTED inspection?

CHAPTER 18

Conclusion

Every subject leader is a manager. Management at any level is concerned with getting things done through other people. The good manager is not one who does it all himself or herself, but one who persuades others to work together to agreed ends. As subject leader you have responsibility for your subject delegated to you and this gives you the authority to undertake the management tasks, but unless you can carry others with you, you will not be able to work effectively.

The good manager needs clear vision. Your work needs to be governed by thought-out ideas about education and about your subject which you are continually developing and modifying in the light of experience and study. These will govern your own practice but you need to select from your own thinking those ideas which will enable you to work most easily with others in any given situation. You need to be always open to other people's ideas and consider them carefully before using or rejecting them. You need to be particularly skilled at drawing out the vision of a group and then drawing the ideas together into a framework which can be put into practice. Those who work with you should feel that they are truly involved and able to contribute to the development of the work of the school.

With successful experience as a leader you will develop confidence in your relationships with adults as well as with children. You need to be sensitive to and caring for others, a good listener who can interpret other people's behaviour and make each person feel that he or she really matters and has something special to contribute. You need to be able to help others in their work, guiding and counselling unobtrusively. You need to be able to deal with complaints and criticism and be skilled at identifying problems. You need strategies for helping others to meet and overcome difficulties, giving them confidence that there can be a satisfactory outcome.

As subject leader you need to be able to work within the constraints of your own situation, knowing your own strengths and limitations and those of others and seeking to complement the skills of other staff. You need to be persuasive but know when to persuade and when to hold back, able to involve others but able to work unobtrusively so that they sometimes believe that they did it all themselves. You need to be skilled at being critical in ways that are positive and supportive. You need to be well organised and demonstrate a high level of self-discipline, providing a role model for others.

You need to be able to withstand pressure because you have a clear sense of direction. You need good analytical skills, but you also need to be able to work intuitively, sensing the way people feel and reacting to them. You need to be creative and inventive, able to generate ideas to deal with new situations.

This is all a counsel of perfection, something to try to live up to rather than a blue-print for the perfect subject leader. It is not an easy task, but it can be a very rewarding one.

Bibliography

Bastide, D. (1999) *Coordinating Religious Education Across the Primary School*, London: Falmer.

Bell, D. and Ritchie, R. (1999) *Towards Effective Subject Leadership in the Primary School*, Buckingham: Open University Press.

Bennis, W. and Nanus, B. (1985) *Leaders*, New York: Harper and Row.

Blandford, S. (1997) *Middle Management in Schools: How to Harmonise Managing and Teaching for an Effective School*, London: Pitman Publishing.

Busher, H. and Harris, A. with Wise, C. (2000) *Subject Leadership and School Improvement*, London: Paul Chapman Publishing.

Cawood, J. and Gibbon, J. (1981) *Educational Leadership: Staff Development*, Goodwood, South Africa: Nasou Ltd.

Collett, R. (1994) 'A multicultural policy for all primary schools' in C. Eric Spear (ed.), *Primary Management and Leadership Towards 2000*, Harlow: Longman.

Dean, J. (1996) *Managing Special Needs in the Primary School*, London: Routledge.

Department for Education and Skills (2001) *Special Educational Needs: Code of Practice*, London: DfES.

Fisher, R. and Ury, W. (1983) *Getting to Yes: Negotiating Agreement Without Giving In*, London: Arrow Books Ltd.

Fleming, P. and Amesbury, M. (2001) *The Art of Middle Management in Schools: A Guide to Effective Subject, Year and Team Leadership*, London: David Fulton Publishers.

Frase, L. and Conley, S. (1994) *Creating Learning Places for Teachers, Too*, Thousand Oaks, California: Corwin Press Inc..

Fullan, M. (1985) 'Change processes and strategies at the local level' in *The Elementary School Journal*, Vol. 85, No. 3, University of Chicago.

Fullan, M. and Stiegelbauer, S. (1991) *The New Meaning of Educational Change*, London: Cassell.

Garrett, V. (1997) 'Managing change' in B. Davies and L. Ellison (eds), *School Leadership for the 21st Century*, London: Routledge.

Glatthorn, A. (1990) *Supervisory Leadership: Introduction to Instructional Supervision*, USA: HarperCollins Publishers.

Glover, D. and Law, S. (1996) *Managing Professional Development*, London: Kogan Page.

Hargeaves, D. H. and Hopkins, D. (1991) *The Empowered School: The*

Management and Practice of Development Planning, London: Cassell.

Hewton, E. (1987) *School Focused Staff Development: Guidelines for Policy Makers*, London: Falmer.

Jackson, K. F. (1975) *The Art of Solving Problems*, London: Heinemann.

Kemp, R. and Nathan, M. (1989) *Middle Management in Schools: A Survival Guide*, Oxford: Blackwell.

Lewin, K. (1938) *The Conceptual Measurement of Psychological Forces*, USA: Duke University Press.

Lewin, K. (1951) *Field Theory and Social Science*, London: Harper.

Lieberman, A. and Miller, L. (eds) (1991) *Staff Development for Education in the 90s: New Demands, New Realities, New Perspectives* (2nd edition) New York and London: Teachers' College Press, Columbia University.

Little, J. (1981) 'The power of organisational setting: school norms and staff development', paper presented at the annual meeting of the American Educational Research Association, Los Angeles.

Loucks-Horsley, S. and Stiegelbauer, S. (1991) 'Using knowledge of change to guide staff development' in A. Lieberman and L. Miller (eds), *Staff Development for Education in the 90s: New Demands, New Realities, New Perspectives* (2nd edition), New York and London: Teachers' College Press, Columbia University.

Macbeath, J. and Myers, K. (1999) *Effective School Leaders: How to Evaluate Your Leadership Potential*, London: Pearson Education for the *Financial Times* and Prentice-Hall.

Mortimore, P., Mortimore, J. and Thomas, H. (1994) *Managing Associate Staff: Innovation in Primary and Secondary Schools*, London: Paul Chapman Publishing Ltd.

Newton, C. and Tarrant, T. (1992) *Managing Change in Schools: A Practical Handbook*, London: Routledge.

Qualifications and Curriculum Authority (1999) *Assessment and Reporting Arrangements Key Stage 2*, London: QCA Publications.

Rodd, J. (1994) *Leadership in Early Childhood: The Pathway to Professionalism*, Buckingham: Open Univeristy Press.

Simmons, J. (1985) 'Exploring changes in teacher thought as they do action research in their classrooms: Strengthening the link between research and practice', paper presented at the annual meeting of the National Staff Development Council, Denver, USA.

Starratt, J. (1995) *Leaders with Vision: The Quest for School Renewal*, California: Corwin Press Inc..

Teacher Training Agency (1998) *National Standards for Subject Leaders*, London: Teacher Training Agency.

Telford, H. (1996) *Transforming Schools through Collaborative Leadership*, London: Falmer.

Terrell, I. (1997) 'Working with people – leadership from the middle' in

M. Leask and I. Terrell (eds), *Development Planning and School Improvement for Middle Managers*, London: Kogan Page.

Wallace, B. (1983) *Teaching the Very Able Child*, London: Ward Lock Educational.

West, N. (1998) *Middle Management in the Primary School: A Development Guide for Curriculum Leaders, Subject Managers and Senior Staff,* London: David Fulton Publishers.

Woodcock M. (1979) *Team Development*, London: Gower.

Wragg, E. C., Haynes, G. S., Wragg, C. M. and Chamberlain, R. P. (2000) *Failing Teachers?,* London: Routledge Falmer.

Index

Also available...

The Art of Middle Management in Primary Schools
A Guide to Effective Subject, Year and Team Leadership

Peter Fleming and **Max Amesbury**

'Strong on management styles and getting the best out of people, the advice on performance management is timely.'

The Teacher

Contents: What is middle management? Different management styles; A look at effective school cultures; Getting the best out of people; Building your team; Effective communication; Meetings; Administration and resource management; Managing change and development; Performance management; Stress management and time management.

£16.00 • Pb • 176 pg • 1-85346-736-7 • 2001

Improving the Quality of Education for All
A Handbook of Staff Development Activities

David Hopkins

| 2nd Edition |

This book provides many practical staff development activities and gives examples of specific changes which have taken place in IQEA schools, relating both to the progress of students and the professional development of their teachers. These training activities and examples demonstrate that improving the quality of education has many facets, not all of which can be measured and translated into league tables.

£25.00 • 144 pg • 1-85346-649-2 • 2002

Performance Management
Monitoring Teaching in the Primary School

Sara Bubb and **Pauline Hoare**

This book offers practical guidance on how to go about performance management. Based on experience of working with schools and running courses, and using the latest research on business strategies appropriate for education. Throughout, the purpose is to help schools and teachers to be more effective.

£17.50 • Pb • 144 pages • 1-85346-740-5 • 2001

The Effective Induction of Newly Qualified Primary Teachers
An Induction Tutor's Handbook

Sara Bubb

This is an excellent insight into the world of induction tutors. The book is optimistic yet realistic, sensitive yet uncompromising, and manages to provide up-to-date guidance on the support, monitoring and assessment aspects of the role. All issues are tackled thoroughly from both the NQT's and the induction tutors perspective, and pros and cons are explained carefully... *The Effective Induction of Newly Qualified Primary Teachers* will undoubtedly make induction tutors' lives easier and this book merits a wide audience from NQTs to headteachers.'

Managing Schools Today

£24.00 • 128 pg • 1-85346-684-0 • 2000

Teacher-Led Development Work
Guidance and Support

David Frost and **Judy Durrant**

The book

- demonstrates how secondary and primary teachers can contribute to the improvement of their school, whilst pursuing their own continued professional development and gaining accreditation through school-based work

- provides guidelines for school managers, higher education tutors, external consultants and LEA advisors establishing school-based support

- gives tried and tested flexible proformas, checklists and other practical tools that are ideal for training, INSET or a personal audit.

£25.00 • 160 pg • 1-84312-006-2 • 2002

Helping Teachers Develop Through Classroom Observation

Diane Montgomery

| 2nd Edition |

'an essential practical guide for teachers and managers, which is easily read and balances theory, experience and practice.'

CPD Update

Contents: Performance management; Classroom observation methods; Case studies in appraisal using the formative system; Effective learning; Effective teaching.

£18.00 • Pb • 192 pg • 1-85346-872-X • 2002

Teaching Assistants
Practical Strategies for Effective Classroom Support

Maggie Balshaw and **Peter Farrell**

This practical book is intended to support schools and LEAs in developing effective strategies for working with teaching assistants. It is related to the DfEE's *Working with Teaching Assistants: A good practice guide* (2000). Suggested approaches are supported with real examples from practice, showing the reality of how schools can review and develop practice and so become more effective in their management and support of teaching assistants.

£16.00 • Pb • 144 pg • 1-85346-828-2 • 2002

Appointing and Managing Learning Support Assistants
A Practical Guide for SENCOs and other Managers

Jennie George and **Margaret Hunt**

Written specially for SENCOs and other managers, this book offers guidance on employing and managing LSAs and all those who support children in mainstream education (LSAs, TAs, SSAs or STAs).

£15.00 • • 112 A4 pages • 1-84312-062-3 • September 2003

David Fulton Publishers, The Chiswick Centre, 414 Chiswick High Road, London W4 5TF
Tel: 020 8996 3610   Fax: 020 8996 3622   E-mail: orders@fultonpublishers.co.uk
www.fultonpublishers.co.uk

Lightning Source UK Ltd.
Milton Keynes UK
UKOW06f1134210814

237312UK00004B/26/P